PENOBSCOT SHAMANISM

BY

FRANK G. SPECK

KRAUS REPRINT CO.
Millwood, New York
1974

Reprinted with the permission of the
American Anthropological Association
KRAUS REPRINT CO.
A U.S. Division of Kraus-Thomson Organization Limited

Printed in U.S.A.

CONTENTS

PENOBSCOT SHAMANISM

By FRANK G. SPECK

INTRODUCTION

THE only feasible way to deal with Penobscot shamanism, which is at bottom not a very complex matter either in theory or in practice, is to discuss the facts, few as they be, that fell under observation while investigating the northeastern tribes, and to present the shamanistic lore in mythology as well as that now current among the Indians.

Concerning our sources, it should be borne in mind at the beginning that most of the Indians of this part of the country still believe more or less in the power of sorcery and witchcraft.[1] Plenty of them also tell of living people whom they have heard are shamans, but those who are thus reported are from remote districts and are known mostly by hearsay. The nearer one comes to the home of a reputed man of magic, the less one hears of him, while in his own village nowadays he is generally denied. This, of course, applies only to the Penobscot. I knew of only one person living at the time of my earlier residence in the village who could in any way be regarded as a shaman and he was esteemed only as a stupid liar in his home village on Indian Island. I shall subsequently give all the information that I can concerning him. The best of our data is, in short, traditional.

Much has to be drawn directly from those exhaustless sources of information on all subjects of early life, the myths. I have consequently used the texts of myths, both in Penobscot and in English, for reference. A few which bear especially upon shamanism have been included in the paper in their original form. And

---

[1] Professor J. D. Prince, "Some Passamaquoddy Witchcraft Tales," *Proceedings, American Philosophical Society*, no. 160, p. 181, and C. G. Leland, *Algonquin Legends of New England*, p. 8, have both remarked in this respect concerning the neighboring tribes.

next, the knowledge and memory of Newell Lyon have been employed on the subject.

A matter all important in any study of the practices of religion or, as we might preferably speak of it, the employment of supernatural power or magic, is the term, in Penobscot, *ktaha'n·do*[1], which has the meaning of "*great manitu.*" The element *-han·do* here appears as the cognate of *manitu* in the Central Algonkian dialects. Its usage in the texts is also similar; the most careful interpreters rendering it as "great magic." It is used generally as an adjective qualifying animate beings and inanimate objects, too, when these are in some way the means of conjury or magical practice.[2] So far Penobscot, Passamaquoddy, and Malecite coincide as regards this term and its significance. In the writer's Penobscot material there is not any instance of its use to denote an independent abstract idea, so we are at a loss how to approach a definition of the concept. As an adjective, it seems to mean mysterious, magical, powerful, miraculous, enabling things to be done supernaturally.

The power of *ktaha'n·do* appears as a source of dynamics which empowers not only the out-and-out mythical personalities but semi-professional magicians even down to the present times. In this it is a conception which, though wanting in definition, becomes functionally similar to the manitu concept discussed by Wm. Jones among the Central Algonkian[3].

Mᴂde'olinu

The Penobscot shaman is denoted by the term *mᴐde'olinu.* Opinion seems to be settled on the derivation of the first part of

---

[1] Malecite and Passamaquoddy *ktahánt* is the corresponding term, Micmac *buówin.*

[2] Illustrations of the use of the term are *ktahán·dwi·álᴐmus* "great magical dog," *ktahán·dwi·nɑgʷzu* "great magic appearing," *madjahán·do* "evil power," "Devil." *elhán·do* "so magical." *nᴐgátc wéwiłe tan udot'hán·dowin* "Then you will know how powerful his magic is." *Man·doa·'mek'ʷ* "Spirit (Devil) fish" Penobscot proper name; *auhan·dosi·s* "little devil," the generic name for insects, *gi·nhán·do* "great (monstrous) magician," *ndalidᴐhɑdámes·in al'han·dówɑŋgan,* "I think I feel myself to have equal magic."

[3] Cf. also A. B. Skinner, *Journal of American Folk-Lore,* vol. XXVIII, no. 109, p. 261, (1915) for Menomini equivalent, "A god, the supernatural power imparted by a god, or the seat of this supernatural power." For Jones, see *ibid.,* vol. XVIII, pp. 183–190.

the term (məde-) from "sound of drumming."[1] While the consciousness of such a derivation is altogether lost in the modern native linguistic knowledge, some confirmation for it may be found in the use of the elements of the term. The translation "drum sound person" suggests itself as an equivalent.[2] The term is simply known as the equivalent of sorcerer, witch, magician, although by analogy from what we know of shamans in the neighboring regions, it may be concluded that part of the shaman's power was thought to lie in his drum. In later literature, however, little or no mention is made of the shaman's drum and this is true even in the myths.

Drums are nevertheless mentioned by the early missionaries as being the property of shamans.[2] The missionaries themselves may have been responsible for the decline of drum-sorcery in later times. We have one specific reference to drum-magic in Passamaquoddy by Professor Prince, who gives the text of a witch song.[3]

[1] J. D. Prince, "Some Passamaquoddy Witchcraft Tales," *Proceedings of American Philosophical Society*, No. 160 (1899), p. 186, comments on the term by saying *m'déaulin* wizard appears in old Delaware as *mete·u* "one who drums," e.g., a witch doctor, referring to the practice of the medicine men of beating drums to drive away evil spirits. Thus Delaware *meteohet* is a drum or any hollow body. In modern Delaware *meteu* denotes a turkey-cock, which drums with its wings (Anthony in Brinton Lenape Legends, p. 83). Cf. Ojibwa *medē'win* "sorcery" and *tewe'ige* "he beats a drum." In another paper Professor Prince says the Passamaquoddy *m'deolinwuk* are "drum beaters" from their methods of exorcism.

In Penobscot the term for drum is *pakhola'ŋgan*, "that which is hollow struck with a stick," Malecite *pagaholágen*, Montagnais *tēwe'hi·gan*, Micmac *dji·gamáɣan* (also *bepkwejedaak*, see Rand Dictionary, p. 92). In the various dialects *made-* denotes "sound" or "noise," Micmac *mide·'du* (See also S. T. Rand, *Micmac Dictionary*, p. 245) while in Penobscot and Malecite *madē-* denotes "the noise of something," for instance *madedónke* "the sound of talking," *madéo's·e* "the sound of walking," (Malecite) *madébagahòlu* "the sound of drumming," *madegan'* "the sound of dancing." It seems that *-ol-* in the term *madéolinu* is the element denoting something hollow, as *n'bagahólan* "I drum." The final element *-inu* is the Penobscot form of the common Algonkian term for "person." While in Penobscot complexes the *aln-*, *alin-* occur (*alnabe* "Indian person") the usual final form in words of this character is *-inu* (*pmáuzowi'no* "living person," *no'peo'sáwino* "warrior," etc.) which makes it more probable that the element *-ol-* in *madéolinu* is to be explained as above.

[2] "Relation of Father Drouillets" (1647), *Jesuit Relations* (Thwaites edition), (vol. XXXI, pp. 193–197).

[3] J. D. Prince, "Notes on Passamaquoddy Literature," *Annals, New York Academy of Sciences*, vol. XIII, no. 4, p. 385. "I sit down and beat the drum, and by the sound

Several specimens of drums have been produced by the Penobscot showing that one type of instrument, at least, resembles in general construction the drums of the tribes north of the St. Lawrence and having the snare string across the head. One of these specimens, 25 cm. in breadth by 90 mm. in thickness, has a head of green deerskin stretched over the hoop of wood. The skin heads are laced irregularly with babiche. A wrapped handle of rawhide is fastened on one side across one face, two strings of babiche (rawhide) are strung to act as snares, while around the opposite side is a row of babiche strings tied so as to represent fringe. The drum-stick is a simple affair of cedar (arbor vitæ) 25 cm. long. The presence of the snare here is interesting, since it is a feature of the drums of Algonkian tribes northward through Labrador.[1] The Penobscot regard the buzzing noise made by the snare as a kind of "singing."

As will be noted in the footnote references, the characteristics of Penobscot shamanism are shared alike by the Abenaki, Wawenock, Malecite, and Passamaquoddy, even in respect to the terms involved.[2] The characteristics, too, are the same in the case of the related Micmac, though here we have a different term designating the shaman.[3] On the whole there is great uniformity in the

of the drum I call the animals from the mountains. Even the great storms harken to the sound of my drum. I sit down and beat the drum and the storm and thunder answer the sound of my drum. The great whirlwind ceases its raging to listen to the sound of my drum. I sit down and beat the drum and the spirit of the night air comes and listens to the sound of my drum. Even the great Wuchowsin will cease moving his wings to harken to the sound of my drum. I sit down and beat the drum and the spirit under the water comes to the surface and listens to the sound of my drum, and the wood spirit will cease chopping and harken to the sound of my drum. I sit down and beat the drum and the great Appodumken will come out of the deep and harken to the sound of my drum. The lightning, thunder, storms, gales, forest spirit, whirlwind, water spirit and spirit of the night air are gathered together and are listening to the sound of my drum."

[1] Specimens collected by the writer from the Montagnais and Naskapi of Southern Labrador for the Museum of the Geological Survey of Canada, the Museum of the American Indian, and the American Museum of Natural History. Cf. also L. Turner, "Ethnology of the Ungava District," *Eleventh Annual Report, Bureau of American Ethnology*, pp. 324–5.

[2] Abenaki (St. Francis) *mədaulinú* and Wawenock, *mədeolenú*, Malecite and Passamaquoddy *m'déulin'*.

[3] Micmac *buówin*. Cf. also "Bouhinne," Leclerq" New Relation of Gaspesia" (Paris, 1691), *Edition of Champlain Society*, Toronto, by W. F. Ganong, 1910, pp.

shamanistic practices of the entire northeast. In the collections of tales, both in the native dialects and in English, which I have made from the different branches of the Wabanaki group, are some tales concerning shamanism proper. For arbitrary reasons place has been made for some of these in this body of material which is otherwise exclusively Penobscot. They supplement the testimony of the footnotes showing that, despite local differences, the body of material in the whole area is practically an idea unit. The Penobscot shaman seems to have been purely a wonder worker whose magic power was derived from the spiritual and the animal world. His chief activity was to overcome rivals and demonstrate wherever he could the superiority of his own strength. From all accounts of their behavior the shamans were heartless egoists. The term shaman here, besides, refers in a modern sense to people who have only weak relations with supernatural forces. The greater the degree of intimacy with the force the greater was their power. Ordinary persons who do things in funny or unexplainable ways are still often humorously called *mǝde'olinu.* In addition to maintaining a general rivalry from village to village and even between neighboring tribes, shamans had the faculty of foretelling events, sending their spirits and helpers abroad to do their bidding or learn what was wanted.

The shaman in the tribe seems to have had all the functions ascribed to sorcerers in the north, that of causing sickness or misfortune, of removing the same, and contesting his power with that of rivals, while occasionally we learn of more altruistic services rendered in warfare and in ridding the world of monsters. Our conclusions, however, as to the character of the shaman and his profession may better be deferred until the available data have been given.

217–223. S. T. Rand, *Legends of the Micmacs*, p. xliii, xliv, gives a concise definition of the term "Booöwin is the Micmac word for wizard. . . . The ancient booöwin could, he (the Micmac) firmly believes, fly through the air, go down through the earth, remain under water as long as he chose, transform himself into an animal." Also, C. G. Leland, *Algonquin Legends of New England*, p. 86, Boo-oinak, magicians. S. Hagar, "Micmac Magic and Medicine," *Journal of American Folk-Lore*, vol. IX, no. 34, p. 173, gives a detailed account of the "booöin, Magic power and all possessors of it."

Although everyone knew the *mǝde'olinu* when he had become famed through his achievements, there is no remembrance of a shaman having been slain for vengeance by the friends of his victims or of his having been attacked on account of his maleficence. This seems a little extraordinary since nearly every mishap and evil consequence in the little native community was in the early times attributed to the action of a shaman whose identity, if not actually known was, we are told, at least generally suspected. As to special public functions, the shamans appear to have had none, except occasionally in the myths as destroyers of tribal enemies, mundane or spiritual, and dispellers of tribal misfortunes.

Family Shamanism

A shamanistic feature of considerable importance now deserves some attention, though we are greatly handicapped by the unavoidable circumstance that our knowledge of it is obscured by antiquity and the decay of the old life. Family shamanism is directly indicated by tradition among the Penobscot. Different family groups, we are told, had their own shamans whose talents were employed in the protection of their family hunting territories against trespassers. A shaman could detect when other hunters were intruding upon his family tract. He could then take measures to thwart and punish the infringement. From this situation arise numerous tales (see pages 23, 29, 35, 64) in which we hear how intruders are discovered in animal guise, in which traps are sprung, hunting trips spoiled by bad luck and the like. The malefactors are then spiritually persecuted by the shaman of the group, who may himself be the proprietor of the territory. One gathers an impression that such a shamanistic function may have been fundamental among a hunting people of this character. Besides the Penobscot tales of this sort we have other references to a similar function in other parts of the northern area. References occur among the Montagnais[1]

---

[1] The writer's Montagnais and Mistassini notes indicate that conjurors had the power of ascertaining by magic means when trespass occurred on their hunting grounds. They sometimes frightened intruders by placing ghosts as guardians at different spots in the districts. Conjurors also caused sickness or bad luck to fall upon persons who trespassed on their hunting grounds.

and among the northern Ojibwa.¹ The feature of family shamanism
is, however, a posterior discovery in the region so we have not as
yet sufficient information to assign to it a continuous distribution
over northern North America.   Nevertheless it may be expected to
be reported from intervening Algonkian tribes and even from the
northwest.   It is of no little significance that the same feature has
analogues among the Paleoasiatic peoples.   Bogoras discusses it and
makes a point of its probable antiquity among the Chukchi.² In
considering, however, the question of distribution we could hardly go
further at present than to remind ourselves of the many positive and
negative similarities between the Athapascans and Algonkians of
northern Canada and the natives of northeastern Asia, not only in
shamanism but in other topics of culture.

MEANS OF ACQUIRING SHAMAN'S POWER

The means of acquiring magic power were considered to be
more or less involuntary according to the Penobscot.

We learn, from Lion,³ that a group of seven or eight men were
known sometimes to have gotten together in a "dark lodge" ⁴
and camp out in this way in a company.   Here they would each
perform tricks after which it would be learned that some perhaps
had acquired magic power and secured some particular *baohi*'*gan*

¹ Cf. "Family Hunting Territories and Social Life of Various Algonkian Bands
of the Ottawa Valley," *Memoir 70, Anthropological Series, No. 8, Geological Survey of
Canada* (1915), p. 4.   "Each family as a rule had some shaman in its ranks who could
be called upon to work malefic influence upon a member of another family who was
known to have intruded (upon the former's hunting grounds).   In this way we can see
how, in the community of old, a much involved system of cross-conjuring must have
grown up often, as the Indians themselves state, causing more or less rivalry and feuds
between certain families.   Sickness in general came to be attributed to these sources
it is claimed."

² W. Bogoras, "The Chukchee (Religion)," *Memoirs of the American Museum of
Natural History*, vol. VII, part 2 (1907), p. 413.   "Family shamanism being quite
simple and primitive probably antedated the shamanism of individuals having special
skill and invention, and the latter seems to have been based on the former.   Family
shamans exist among the Koryak, Asiatic Eskimo, and probably existed also among
the Kamchadal and Yukaghir."

³ Newell Lion was one of the principal contributors to our information on early
Penobscot life.   He lost his life in the woods in the spring of 1919.

⁴ *bəsəgi'k·an* "dark wigwam," a small conical brush wigwam.

or helper (see p. 249). To ordinary people the *mɔde'olinu* was, and still is, extremely mysterious. No one professes to know just how any shaman first obtained his power or even how he operated it. In the minds of most of these Indians, I think, the shaman is thought to have acquired power involuntarily, presumably to have been born with it or to have had it grow on him.[1] The same impression is to be gathered from some of the myths and anecdotes. Folklore incidentally claims that to have stains in one's nether garments is a sure sign of the possession of shamanistic power. Some individuals are even supposed to possess it without knowing that they do. As to heredity, there are no general observations; the prevalent idea would indicate that shamans develop, perhaps through some supernatural selection of which they are but the passive instruments.

As to sex we have mention of both male and female *mɔde'olinu*,[2] the latter having the designation *mɔde'olinɑs·kwe* "shaman woman," and, according to the opinion of men, being the more virulent manifestation.

Shamanistic power also seems to have been capable of disintegration and loss. In the myths we learn of heroes using up their power and having to rest and recuperate. This feature is discussed

---

[1] C. G. Leland, *Algonquin Legends of New England*, p. 340, makes a similar statement concerning the Passamaquoddy. He also says that it is sometimes acquired (p. 343) through training. Again (p. 367) the method is by fasting and abstinence from sleep. S. Hagar, *Journal of American Folk-Lore*, vol. IX, no. 34, p. 172, describes how the Micmac believe magic power can be acquired. The novice must keep his object a secret while camping alone in the woods with an outfit for two, the other, an invisible companion. A being will finally appear, it is thought, who will give him the gift of magic, the power to assume animal shapes, to walk through fire unharmed, through water without being drowned, to translate himself through the air with the quickness of thought, to control the elements, to walk on the water, and the like. The idea of contracting to trade oneself for the gift of magic comes out in Micmac through a tale in the writer's collection where a man agrees to pay it with his next boy baby. His next baby is a girl. So he is claimed by his spirit master for which the Micmac find proof in the violent death which he suffered. His body was burned by his relatives. A Malecite informant said that he had heard that if a Christian omitted saying his prayers for seven days and nights he would become a shaman.

[2] Cf. also for Passamaquoddy statement, C. G. Leland, *Algonquin Legends of New England*, p. 342, and S. T. Rand, *Micmac Dictionary*, p. 245. The Micmac of Nova Scotia, according to late chief Abe Toney, believed that the shamans were mostly women.

again on page 267.   Conversion from shamanism is known not alone through missionary testimony but from the evidence of folklore. The renunciation of power seems to have been accompanied by great physical disturbance and even danger of death.   Several anecdotes in Penobscot (p. 265) illustrate this very widespread concept.

INDICATIONS OF THE EXISTENCE OF A SHAMAN'S SOCIETY

If there ever did exist any organized society of shamans in this region the only vestiges of it now are to be found in a few traditional items, which might perhaps indicate the former existence of some-thing of this nature though they do not specify anything definite at all.   The generally unorganized state of society among the Wabanaki tribes appears to have been unbroken by the occurrence of any shamans' association if we decide to rely upon the significance of the evidence that we actually possess.   Such references to shamans' gatherings may denote occasional assemblages for con-tests of power, for tribal protection or for other temporary social purposes and in this light I think we see the true significance of the few accounts of the sessions.   Shamanism, in the region, was prob-ably as much an individualized a matter as religion or the hunt and other features of ethnology.   In the small collection of texts at the end of this paper are given several narratives of this class, one a Penobscot tale of a shamans' assembly for the testing of power, another is the account in Wawenock, a dialect very closely related to Penobscot, of a contest in the exhibition of power (p. 285). After questioning informants and searching through literature, only the following additional mentions are forthcoming.   One is war-ranted, I think, in feeling that here in the northeast no regular society, comparable to the shamans' cults of the Central Algon-kian, held prominence in the life of this region.

According to Nicolar[1] there seems to have been, during one former period at least, a sort of organization among the shamans. Some were appointed, as told in tradition, to follow and watch the first white people seen in the Penobscot country.   We have, how-

---

[1] Joseph Nicolar, *The Red Man*, Bangor, Me., 1896, p. 107 *et passim*.

ever, even from Nicolar no very detailed account of the more secret side of shamanism. Some interesting generalities, however, deserve quotation.

The spiritual men (mǝde'olinu), when closely cornered would disappear on the spot; at other times only some swift-footed animal could be seen leaving the spot, while others would turn into birds and fly away. Although the shamans had been told never to use their power in taking life, in pain of losing it, yet many times this was disregarded, and one shaman would chase another, overtake him and slay him. His remains never would be found because the slayer never told how it was done.

Also, in one of the stories of civil strife among these northern tribes where the opposing shamans were selected to carry on the battle or lead their bands,

the leaders or spiritual men met first and very often without giving orders to their men plunged headlong into the battle using all the power that was in them while the rest would be looking on. They were able to disappear in an instant, and when one conquered he would be seen coming toward his men. . . . In the early days the power of the shamans was not alike, there were some who could see a long distance, and others who could hear a long way, some could send their voices through the air to any distance, while others had the power in their war cry or yell to take away the strength of those they intended to disable so they fall to the ground and lay helpless for some moments.[1]

In regard to the formation of these shaman bands, it seems that they were selected by the chiefs, and furthermore that dissenting or jealous bands grew up to oppose the selected ones. Once at least in the traditional history of the tribe, we hear of a disruption and war resulting from this.[2]

A final isolated account states that a dance of the medicine-men used to occur in the spring of the year when they returned from hunting.

The above reference might be regarded as having some allusion to a shaman society like the Midewin of the Central Algonkian, but there is not much evidence to warrant this since it appears to have been a temporary banding together, more for military than religious ends. No further suggestion of a society of shamans of the typical Algonkian sort is met with in the Penobscot region.

---

[1] Nicolar, op. cit., p. 116.

[2] Ibid., p. 108.

The individual independence of the shamans results in a great deal of specialization in their behavior and in their tricks, so that only the few general facts set down above seem to apply to them as a class. For the rest they have to be considered as separate personages, having their own peculiar attributes for which it is necessary to refer to the collection of anecdotes and shaman stories.

THE BAOHI·'GAN

Every magician had his helper which seems to have been an animal's body into which he could transfer his state of being at will. The helper was virtually a disguise, though we do not know whether the animal was believed to exist separately from the shaman when not in the shaman's service or whether it was simply a material form assumed by the shaman when engaged in the practice of magic. The helper then is known by the term *baohi·'gan*, a very interesting term which may be explained as meaning "instrument of mystery."

The Penobscot stem *bao-*, which I believe denotes the concept of mystery, is common property in some capacity to most of the northeastern tribes.[1] In Penobscot the stem evidently appears again in the term *nəbau'linu* "mystery man" described as a puzzle maker whose speech was couched in symbolism or allegory. These men, a few of whom are remembered by older members of the living generation, posed as sages. Their utterances were considered too profound to be understood except after careful thought. They not only spoke at council meetings but frequently practised their art for amusement. Mechling evidently refers to similar men among the Malecite[2] and Leland defines *n'paowlin* among the Passamaquoddy[3] as a man learned in mysteries, a scholar, comparable to Micmac *buo'win* pow-wow man.

A strict correspondence between the naming and functions of

---

[1] Micmac *buo-*, Malecite and Passamaquoddy *pu-*, Abenaki *bao-*, Natick *pow-*, (J. H. Trumbull, "Natick Dictionary," *Bulletin 25, Bureau of American Ethnology*, p. 124.)

[2] W. H. Mechling, *Malecite Tales*, p. 18, footnote.

[3] C. G. Leland, *Algonquin Tales of New England*, p. 352, footnote. The Malecite term *nəpáulin* means a "learned man" in modern usage.

the animal helper exists only among the Penobscot and Passamaquoddy and Malecite.[1] Except for the dissimilarity of the designating term (Micmac *nti·o'm*, *nti·o'mel*, third person) we could
also include in this grouping the Micmac, among whom the tales
of the exploits of shamans and their helpers are almost identical
throughout with those of the Penobscot, Malecite, and Passamaquoddy.

The variation of the animal helper idea among the tribes north
of the St. Lawrence who form the culture area corresponding to
that south of the river, is very interesting. The animal disguise
of the shaman here seems to be a less emphatic feature if we may
conclude from the nature of the information presented by pub-
lished sources. Skinner says of the Cree:[2]

> Evil conjuring is performed by *miteo* against his rivals or enemies. A
> dream informs him what course to take. Sometimes a bird or animal is *captured*
> and imbued with malevolent power. It is sent to the intended victim and strikes
> or falls upon him, killing him.

The Montagnais, as I have learned, also dream of the visit of some
particular animal whose advice received in the dream is followed
for the procuring of game.[3] In the lower St. Lawrence the Montagnais of Escoumains believe that the shaman has a black bird
which he consults for supernatural knowledge and which he may
also send away on spiritual errands. Concerning the Naskapi, Turner
says something similar.[4]

---

[1] Passamaquoddy and Malecite *pu·'hi·gan*. In Micmac the term corresponding
to the *baohi·'gan* of the three tribes just mentioned is *nti·óm*, first personal form
(*utió·mel*, third person).

Cf. also S. T. Rand, *Legends of the Micmacs*, p. 133, "His teomul is the loon
whose form and habits he immediately assumes," and p. 161, "sundry animals passed
by . . . all of them animals and brutes which were at the same time men who had
the power of assuming the form of their tutelary deities, their teomuls," and p. 12,
"Booöin as tutelar deity of Chepichkam" (snail). See also Rand, *Micmac Dictionary*,
p. 267, "totem-ootooömul."

[2] Alanson B. Skinner, "Notes on the Eastern Cree and Northern Saulteaux,"
Anthropological Papers of the American Museum of Natural History, vol. IX, part I,
(1911), p. 67.

[3] Cf. F. G. Speck, "Game Totems of Northeastern Algonkians," *American Anthro-
pologist*, N.S., vol. XIX, no. I (1917), p. 16.

[4] L. M. Turner, "Ethnology of the Ungava District," *Eleventh Annual Report*,
Bureau of American Ethnology, p. 272. "Each person has a patron spirit. . . . These

Direct information from Penobscot informants says that the *baohi·'gan* could be sent to fight or to work for his master the shaman.[1] It could be sent on any mission whatsoever according to the shaman's will. We are told, too, that the owner remained inert while his *baohi·'gan* was away.

Whatever injury was done to the *baohi·'gan* in an encounter, was transferred to the shaman owner.[2] If it were killed the owner died simultaneously. We have several direct cases of the mention of how shamans were slain through the destruction or wounding of their helpers. Including dream instances, (p. 269–71) there may be noted three cases where the *baohi·'gan* was killed by a blow with a stick on the head, and two in which a jab from a stick encompassed their end. Recovery in such a case could only be had by the administration of medicine given by the causer.[3]

The *baohi·'gan* when acquired by a shaman was thenceforth considered, said Newell Lion, as a part of himself. Accordingly we find certain taboos existing governing the shaman's relation to it. Another term used in referring to the *baohi·'gan* is "his helper in trouble."

---

spirits assume an infinite variety of forms and to know just what form it assumed when it inflicted its baneful effects, the shamans or medicine-men must be consulted."

[1] An excellent illustration, and an analogy as well is furnished in a Malecite tale related by Gabe Perley. Sapiel Sockalexis, a former shaman, engaged in a magic contest with Newell Paul. Paul was at Woodstock, N. B., and Sockalexis was at French village. Their *buhi·'gan* (Malecite) were pitted against each other. Sockalexis was in his room groaning and evidently undergoing severe exertion. His wife heard the struggle but did not interfere, or intrude. At last he came forth and showed her a beetle (*mi·kənákwəs*, species of "June bug" called " turtle ") which he had captured and placed in a glass. He had tied its legs together with fine hair. "I got him, I got him!" he declared. Paul's *buhi·'gan* was the beetle.

[2] The Micmac analogy is found in S. T. Rand, *Legends of the Micmacs*, p. 12. The chief, a shaman or booöin, dies when his teömul (tutelar deity) is killed. This is also confirmed by Micmac informants in Nova Scotia.

Strictly analogous stories, some of them almost identical with ones given here, are recorded among the Iroquoian tribes. I have not tried systematically to collect these but the following sources may be consulted. E. A. Smith, "Myths of the Iroquois," *Second Annual Report, Bureau of American Ethnology*, 1880–1, pp. 72–3–4. E. W. Connelley, *Wyandot Folk-Lore*, p. 100–1, also C. M. Barbeau, *Huron and Wyandot Mythology*, 1 p. 348. Also Mohegan, cf. F. G. Speck, "Notes on the Mohegan and Niantic Indians," *Anthropological Papers of the American Museum of Natural History*, vol. III, p. 196 (1909).

[3] Also a Malecite belief (Gabe Perley).

252   AMERICAN ANTHROPOLOGICAL ASSOCIATION   [MEMOIRS, 6

Among the various animal forms, "some being land and others water creatures," assumed by shamans we find by glancing over the available Penobscot material, both in serious myths and in the minor tales relating to recent times, the following guises: otter (3),[1] beaver (2), muskrat, porcupine, white bear, white owl, mink, loon, white loon, bird, eel, snail, bear, panther, dog, spider, ball of fire, bull, wolf, big snake (2), body like a snake with scars on cheeks, windfall, and person playing on Jew's harp.[2]

A shaman usually had but one "*baohi·'gan*," but John Neptune, who was a powerful magician, according to Mr. Ferris'[3] information, had seven.

Some of the tribe followed John Neptune one day until he stopped by the shore of a lake. There he sang and sang until an immense eel arose from the water and making its way to the shore crawled to where John Neptune stood. He took its head between his hands and stroked it softly, thus cementing the bond between them as master and servant. The wolf, the beaver, and the bear were some of his other servants and he would never hurt them nor eat their flesh.

A sample of the kind of first-hand anecdote concerning the *baohi·'gan* related to-day at Oldtown is the following.

I was hunting up in the country by the waters of the St. John River. One night a tremendous ball of fire appeared rushing through the air moving upstream. It had a large head and behind was a snake-like body. I could even see scars on the cheek of the creature. Pretty soon another appeared. I thought they were "fire creatures," *eskuda'hit*, but my father said they must be *mədeoli'nuwak*.

Newell Lion told Mr. Ferris the following:

The usual way for a witch-man to secure his animal helper was to go out in the woods or by the shore of a lake according to the home of the animal and sing to it. Gradually it would appear and then the witch-man would stroke it with his hand in order to bind the animal to him as a servant.

In another instance it is related how one time a shaman went off alone into the woods taking with him a toad which he changed into a woman to afford him companionship during his hunting trip.

---

[1] The figures here denote the number of instances recorded.

[2] Practically all of these are similarly assigned to Malecite and Passamaquoddy shamans. In addition I have tales in Micmac where the creature was a jellyfish (*sasáp·*) and a cat.

[3] Mr. R. H. Ferris, a student in the Department of Anthropology, University of Pennsylvania, undertook to study Penobscot shamanism with Newell Lion while he was visiting the writer in Philadelphia in 1914.

In the memory of the oldest people at Oldtown several *məde'olinu*, with the names of their *baohi·'gan*, are remembered. The most famous of these was Gov. John Neptune whose *baohi·'gan* was an eel *(naha'mu)*. He figures frequently in our data. Another man, Mitchell Francis, a Passamaquoddy who lived much of his life at Oldtown and died there, had a wolf *(ma'lsəm)* for his. He figures in one of the anecdotes.

Certain taboo relationships existed between the man and his *baohi·'gan*. The shaman never killed the animal, nor did he tell even its name nor mention the thing at all. Nevertheless everyone knew the *baohi·'gan* of each noted shaman. Not only did the witch men, moreover, never kill this animal but they would not partake of its flesh when killed by another.

This was the test for discovering the *baohi·'gan* of a witch-man; for if all were at table and the meat of a beaver, for example, was passed around and an individual refused to eat of it everyone knew immediately that the beaver was this man's *baohi·'gan*.[1]

Some shamans are said to have used figures of their animal helpers cut out of birch bark in their performances. These, it is claimed, could be sent abroad on their errands.

Animal helpers distinct from the *baohi·'gan*, are of frequent mention in the myths. They seem, however, to be only volunteer helpers, who take a temporary interest in the fate of the human hero, though some of them promise to render aid again, if need be, when summoned by a wish. In this category we hear of rabbit, dog, porcupine and chickadee several times, and kingfisher, deer, bear, woodchuck, shark, heron, and other anthropomorphic supernatural creatures, such as Thunder, Morning Star, *Mi·'kamwe''s·u*, *Ske'gədemu`s*, and "old man" and "old woman."

The following table is arranged for convenience to show the cognate shamanistic terms in the languages of the Wabanaki tribes and some of their neighbors and culture relatives. Where the sources are not mentioned the information is derived from the writer's fieldnotes.

---

[1] In the words of Newell Lion.

TABLE OF SHAMANISTIC TERMS IN NORTHEASTERN ALGONKIAN DIALECTS

	Penobscot	St. Francis Abenaki	Malecite and Passama-quoddy	Micmac	Montagnais	Mohegan (Southern New England)
Magic power, Sorcery ...	ktahán·do		ktahan't'	buówinu'-'di (booöin-wadagan[1])	mɑnit'o	múndu[2] (Natick, monetu-onk pauwau-onk)
Shaman.....	mədéolinu	mədáulinu[3]	mədéolin[4]	buówin	wabi·'nu[5] kamɑ-ntoci't[6]	moigú (Natick, pauwau, maunêtu)
Animal spiri-tual helper	baohi'gan		puhi·'gan	nti·óm "my-"[7] uti·ómel "his-"		
Fetish in general . :.	wulelmu-[8] gwéwɑŋ-gan	madaǫ́do[9]	wulelmúg-wewàgən[8]	ebat·ɛ'gəm	wewélci-pèlcwagan	

THE TRANSITIONAL PERIODS OF THE SHAMANS

Stories of magicians' exploits fall into three groups which afford an interesting insight into the question of how the whole field of information concerning the practice of personal magic, as an ancient mythological doctrine, has survived in a continually weakening state from the mythical flourishing age through the historical stage

[1] S. T. Rand, *Micmac Dictionary*, p. 245. booöwinode.

[2] The same means the "devil" in Micmac. Here it also means " God." For the Natick terms see J. H. Trumbull, *Bulletin 25, Bureau of American Ethnology*, p. 120, and 64.

[3] See Abenaki text, p. 283.

[4] Malecite and Micmac have still another designation *gi·'nap* which has been defined to me as a "warrior," a "brave," not necessarily a magician. (See also W. H. Mechling, *Malecite Tales*, p. 20, and footnote, and p. 125. "The *ginap* differs from medeolin in that his magical power is not restricted to warlike deeds.")

[5] The *wabi 'nu* ("seeing man") is generally a member of a specific grade of shamans among the Central Algonkian who possess the graded Medicine Lodge (Midewin).

[6] Literally " one who deals with snakes " at Escoumains on the St. Lawrence. The animal helper of the shaman is known as *kamɑdzi't* " one who does evil."

[7] Cf. S. T. Rand, *Legends of the Micmacs*, p. 133; also S. T. Rand, *Micmac Dictionary*, p. 267, who gives it as "teomul." The stem here shorn of its pronominal and intervocal elements is simply -*i·om*.

[8] Literally, "good luck implement."

[9] Cf., A. Maurault, *Histoire des Abenakis* (Quebec, 1866), p. 29 and 122.

down to the period when magical performances are still ascribed to men who are either recently dead or living at a distance. In any case their deeds in consequence cannot be discredited by any but the most skeptical, of whom, of course, there are always a few in regard to all matters of belief among the natives. Corresponding to the three chronological type periods in the history of the shamans we have the following categories of tales as a basis for our viewpoint. First, there are the regular mythical tales of every class (p. 257–9) in which the characters in the narrative transform themselves into animals upon any occasion. It is as though this undifferentiated human-animal character were a normal condition in what may be fittingly termed the mythological age. Secondly there are the specific quasi-historical tales of magicians (pp. 259 *et seq.* and 282) who may even be remembered by name; tales with no other object in view than the relation of a magic act. These belong to the transitional historic period. And thirdly, there are the stories which generally appear as short anecdotes (p. 264, 5) not having the mythological literary qualities at all. These describe the behavior of some individual who either is regarded as possessing magic power by reason of certain mysterious deceptions which may be ascribed to him. These are anecdotes of very recent times, which we might term mere fragmentary units of shaman lore.

It would seem then that in these modern skeptical days the belief in the power of the shaman only lingers in the mind of the Indian as a survival, there being, to his knowledge, no practical basis for it except through hearsay and through mythology. It seems, moreover, as though these beliefs properly belong in the mythological material from whence they have emanated. In both shamanism and mythology the interchangeability of man and certain animals is an essential element. The mythical age is, indeed, virtually an age of universal shamanism[1] which has been trending toward dissolution as time comes down to the present. In the case of the Penobscot the dissolution of shamanistic practice

---

[1] C. G. Leland, *Algonquin Legends of New England*, pp. 284–289, shared the same opinion concerning the Micmac and Passamaquoddy when he speaks of the heroes of mythology in general as *m'teolin*, and again p. 246, and p. 126, where Gluskap transformed some powerful enemy *m'teolin* into sharks.

is about complete, for they can not now boast of a single performer. The last possible claimant to this distinction died a few years ago. His character was so colorless, so unemphatic, and his performances so childish to the minds of his contemporaries that we may wonder whether he was strictly in his sound senses, and as such whether he is to be estimated as a shamanistic character or a mere imbecile. (See anecdotes of Edmund Francis, p. 267.)

Mᴈde'olinu Exploits

We have the following specific magical acts attributed to magicians among the Penobscot. These have been listed from myths in my collection of texts, from specific shaman anecdotes which are given with this paper, and from direct tradition. In some cases the latter is so brief that we are told nothing more than that a *mᴈde'olinu* was once discovered to have done this or that. The category of exploits will, of course, be extended with the increase in amount of tradition and mythology that will be collected in the future. Even as it stands, however, the list shows the general character of the Penobscot shaman's feats and, moreover, it shows that the same general episodes occur in the tales of the related neighboring tribes. We find accordingly that shamans are accredited with the power to kill or injure creatures by pointing the finger at them, to prove their strength over rivals either in combat or in contest, to escape from their enemies by magic means, to spy on enemies, to imprint their footprints in hard surfaces, to increase or diminish their size, to spoil the luck of trappers and hunters, to cause thick ice to heave, to pass through barriers (doors and the like), to roll away a heavy rock, to lift themselves from the floor, to foresee the approach of strangers, to remain beneath water, to force rivals to throw off their animal disguises, to render themselves invisible, and so on.

Among the more conservative northern and central Algonkian tribes shamans are almost inseparably associated with their drums. For some reason in this region, however, we hear little of the shaman's drum, though whether it be on account of deculturation I cannot say. We hear only occasionally through direct tradition of another mechanical aid employed; a flute of cedar wood possessing the power to call game animals and helpers, to attract the affections of women, and to lure enemies into an ambush. This instrument is called *bi·'bi·giwǫdi.*, "*bi·bi·* (onomatopoetic) tube."

In the myths we learn that a belt served frequently as an instrument of magic. Gluskap had one with which he girded on his magic power, so to speak.[1] At different times in the myths such objects as a ball or a pipe[2] are animated temporarily with the sorcerer.

It would hardly seem essential to the discussion of the shaman to mention all the instances which we possess in the collection of texts, of the various exploits involving acts of magic which fall under the classification of shamans' deeds. A few such, however, chosen from the texts, may help to define the feeling toward shamanism which the Indians have today derived from their knowledge of mythology.

Among the most important myth cycles here those of *Gluskǫ'be*, *Kwun·a·'wus*, *Mi·'kamwe's·u*, *Bi·'tes* and others, are to be included in the category of records of magic, the same as those of historic shamanistic personages. Magician tests come into a great many of the myths.

Often when a strange hero—generally an abandoned boy who grows rapidly into a prodigy—comes to the village he is tested by the resident village magicians.

Mythology in fact seems full of the idea that in early times every stranger was a potential magical antagonist. In almost every instance a meeting between the hero of the tale and some other personage results in a contest of shamanistic power. Again, when stories describe how families occupy neighboring camps, we soon find that their innocent friendship endures only until an opportunity offers itself for one to magically tyrannize the other. From the import of the myths, one could wonder whether the old Indian families were ever free from suspicion of malice toward

---

[1] Cf. C. G. Leland, *Algonquin Legends of New England*, p. 86, for a similar Micmac reference.

[2] S. T. Rand, *Legends of the Micmacs*, p. 295, "He (Gluskap) was a great magician and one of his principal sources of power was the pipe."

each other.   In this setting, then, we seem to find the greater part of Wabanaki mythology to be shamanistic in character.

In one case the hero, White Weasel, brings a whale's tail into camp to eat and another shaman at a challenge takes it away. Then he tears this shaman's arm from its socket with one twist. A wrestling match follows in which White Weasel throws his opponent in such a manner that every time he sinks up to his knees in a stone ledge.   Finally he breaks off his legs and kills him.[1] He also drags a great rock, makes a canoe of it, lures his enemies on to it, and blows them to sea to drown, then transforms the village into a sumach bed.

In another tale a hero named Fast Runner is given a test in which he is to break a great bone by twisting it with his two hands.[2] He races with miraculous speed.   The hero later is placed where he is to spear a beaver.   He outruns his rival brothers-in-law, turns himself into a beaver which none of them can spear except the youngest.   Later he assumes the form of a bear, and kills his brothers-in-law.   He also undergoes the freezing test and overcomes his opponents by causing them to freeze to death.[3]   The wrestling test is also on record, while tests in running are mentioned several times.   Another case of test occurs in a tale where White Bear (*Wampsk'ʷ*) whose *baohi·'gan* was a white bear died when the latter was killed.   A hero named White Owl kills him by shooting his heart which, his only vulnerable spot like Achilles, was in his heel.

Gluskabe, the major transformer personage, is regarded as the chief of shamans.   Among the shamanistic feats which he performs is the reduction in size of the moose and the squirrel, the subjugation of the grasshopper, the fox and other animals and things, such as wind, waterfalls, and winter-man.   He makes a canoe of rock, overcomes rivals in the endurance of cold and smoking contests with the magic pipe, in the bowl game contest with magic bowl, lifting a great stone dish, and besides he gives power to Turtle to jump over a wigwam, to win a race, ballgame, and so on.

---

[1] See also page 263 and footnotes.

[2] For the Micmac correspondence see S. T. Rand, "*Legends of the Micmacs*," p. 275.

[3] This was a common popular game, a beaver tibia being used.

Another hero, *Kwun'a'wus*, endures the freezing test and freezes his enemies, runs a rapids in a canoe where his enemies drown, wins a lacrosse game by transforming a spruce twig into a ball, but is finally killed by a female shaman who causes him to be crushed between two mountains. Such are some of the general characteristics of mythical magicians for which there are cognates in practically all the tribes of the group.

In another myth two monster cannibals, shamans of the mythical age, become engaged in a fight in which they employ the power of their voices as weapons. The hero of the tale is warned by his companion to stop up his ears while they pass by lest he succumb to the terrible cries.[1]

Again we learn of the power of shamans to render themselves invisible. (See page 261.) It is attributed to Gluskabe in a myth which relates how he escaped from the amorous pursuit of a female creature (*Pukadji'nskwe's'u*[2]). The same power is attributed to shamans by Nicolar,[3] and we hear of it from general sources among the Indians.

Our material seems to be a little one-sided in respect to the function exercised by the shamans as healers of disease. There are instances of shamans causing disease and injury and of their curing the troubles which they have caused, but we have few or none where the shaman is specifically a doctor. Our evidence for this sort of service on the part of the shamans is only indirect among the

---

[1] Cf. C. G. Leland, *Algonquin Legends of New England*, p. 340–1, and 239, for Passamaquoddy instances of the voice feat. It is also mentioned of the Abenaki. Cf. *Kuloskap The Master*, C. G. Leland and J. D. Prince, New York, 1902, p. 242. Another reference to this belief among the Passamaquoddy is given in footnote 2, on page 263 of this paper, and W. H. Mechling (*Malecite Tales*, p. 76) records one in Malecite. Another account, from Gabe Perley, relates how a former Malecite shaman (Sapiel Sockalexis) claimed the power of sending his voice over great distances. He desired once to wager $25 with Perley that he could yell so that he would be heard from Tobique 110 miles away. Unfortunately for us, Perley was so discreet as to decline the challenge.

[2] Cf. also W. H. Mechling, *Malecite Tales*, p. 123.

[3] Invisibility seems to be an attribute of the Malecite shaman. A tale is related of Sockobi Atwin wherein he was called to aid a woman suffering great pain. He ran forth and later came back in an exhausted condition. "I have fixed her," he said, and then told how he had perceived an invisible witch prod the patient with a stick. He had pursued and driven the witch off, whereupon the pain left the sufferer.

Penobscot, though it frequently occurs in the literature of the other Wabanaki tribes.[1] Among the Penobscot, in recent times, doctors who form a special class of professionals called *nutsi''pi'lewet* "one who cures," have used almost exclusively the practical means of curing, through herbs, roots, bark, leaves, berries, and similar things, in their trade.[2] Some few fetishes have also been found in use, generally preserved among the stores of herbal remedies, with the object of lending strength both to the doctor and to the material means. A perforated stone having a string attached to it has been known to serve in this capacity. In the old accounts of the tribes of Maine mention is made of the same practice and the same fetish. So we have a somewhat satisfactory confirmation of our modern data despite their scantiness.[3] These fetishes were termed *madaodo* (Penobscot *madjahɑ'n·do* "evil power"). There are now in the tribe no prominent professional healers. Sockalexis, said to have been the last medicine man, died about twenty years ago. The herb practitioner never played the part of magician or conjurer, nor was he held in fear.

The ability to recognize another shaman engaged in mischief-making in his animal disguise, and to encompass his end by killing the creature, is frequently attributed to the *mǝde'olinu*. This form

---

[1] The older writers on the Micmac seem to emphasize the shaman's function as a healer. Leclercq (1691), "New Relation of Gaspesia," *Edition of Champlain Society*, Toronto, 1910, by Dr. W. F. Ganong, pp. 217, 223, 299. Also Nicholas Denys (1672), "Description and Natural History of the Coasts of North America," same series, edition by W. F. Ganong (1908), p. 417.

[2] A list of northeastern Algonkian pharmacopeia is given by the writer in a paper entitled "Medicine Practices of the Northeastern Algonquians," *Proceedings of the Nineteenth International Congress of Americanists*, December, 1915.

[3] A. Maurault, *Histoire des Abenakis*, Quebec, 1866, p. 122 says: "Each Indian got various objects from the shamans like little stones, bones or similar things which they preserved. . . . These were called madaodos. They thought that they protected them from accidents and misfortunes and brought them good luck in the hunt, games and warfare." Also Father Drouilletes (cf. *Jesuit Relations*, vol. XXXI (1647), p. 191) says of the Indians of the Kennebec that they kept stones and other things "as a token of dependence upon the Demon, in order to be happy in the hunt, in play or in war. It is given them by some sorcerer or they dream that they will find it in some place, or their imagination makes them believe that the Manitou presents to them whatever they encounter." This belief still prevails in the region; the modern Indians call an object which is suddenly encountered *géskǝmǝzi'*, "something found by chance," and occasionally cherish it as a fetish.

of tale is very common not only throughout the whole northeast but in Iroquoian folklore as well. We have several Penobscot tales of this character (see pages 252 and 287) and a number from the neighboring related tribes.[1]

A Penobscot example is the following:

> The Indians were camping on the St. John river and living on eels which they were spearing through the ice. One day a white loon appeared suddenly. After this the spears of the eel catchers struck only rock instead of mud and of course there were no eels. The shaman in the camp told them that the white loon was a mischievous French magician who must be killed. The hunters killed the loon and immediately afterwards the eeling became all right again.

An account of a typical shamans' exploit of a similar nature is the following anecdote told at Oldtown.

> One night some hunters were camping in a wigwam near some friends. During the night an otter appeared at the doorway and one of the men in the bed at the back of the lodge opposite the door began talking in his sleep. One of the hunters awakened, seized a brand from the fire and poked the otter which ran out. A noise as of someone running away was immediately afterward heard outside. They went out and there lay the otter dead, surrounded by a kind of hoar frost, near the wind break or fence of brush which encircled the camp. The next season the same band camped at the same place and two boys of the band ran to a well to get a bucket of water. One of the boys got the pole of the well bucket stuck in his side. He staggered right over to the brush fence at the same spot where the otter had died, and a frost gathered round him. In the morning he was dead, lying in the same spot. They all thought that he was the *mǝde'olinu* who had appeared as an otter the year before. It was an uncanny affair.[2]

Charlie (Daylight) Mitchel told how his father was once hunting up on the Penobscot waters, and came under the influence of a *mǝde'olinu*, a woman named Caribou-quarter from *Mɑtnǫ'guk*.[3] He could catch nothing in his traps. Every time he visited them he found a stick stuck in them and the traps sprung. One night, however, he heard someone invisible playing on a jew's harp across on the other side of his fire. He took a sharp stick and fixed it near the fire. The next night when he heard the playing he

---

[1] Also Abenaki, *Kuloskap the Master*, C. G. Leland and J. D. Prince, p. 244. A shaman in the form of a muskrat is killed by a Mohawk shaman. In another tale (*ibid.*, p. 250), a similar contest is waged between shamans in the guises of bat, snowy owl, and wolverine.

[2] Related by Old Joe Francis.

[3] This is the uppermost village of the Penobscot on an island opposite Lincoln, Me.

thrust forward with it and struck something. The next morning his hunting luck was all right again. He returned home to the village with plenty of fur after a successful trip. Shortly after his return he learned that a woman at *Matnᵫ'guk* was suffering from a wound. She soon died and everyone said that she was a *mᵊde'olinu*, the one who had annoyed Mitchel in the woods.[1]

Chief among the shamans' activities seem to have been the waging of feuds between one another for causes which are far from certain; seemingly for little more than the demonstration of their power or for subduing rivals, or from fancied offence, jealousy or trespass.

The shaman is referred to as having the power of inflicting injury and even death upon the object of his temper by pointing at him with the forefinger and saying *"Katci· kdli·na'mi·'tun djen·i·'."* You! You will see something before long!

This imprecation was sufficient to scare the victim and to result either in steps for the placation of the offended shaman or else in the physical decline of the victim through obsessive fear. Merely having been "crossed," in the Indian-English vernacular meaning "contradicted or displeased," was a sufficient basis for such malevolent, possibly hypnotic action. Other anecdotes in this category are as follows:

A party of hunters out in a canoe happened to have a shaman among them. Some ducks came flying over. The hunters said that they wished they could get some, although the flock was out of range. The shaman thereupon pointed his finger at the birds, and every time he did so a duck fell dead. Johnny Susup's story.

Whenever a shaman grew angry at anyone or was disappointed at being refused something by a certain man he stretched out his arms pointing with his index finger at the person and said, "You will regret it." Shortly afterwards the person either died of some foul disease or was found in the woods cut and bleeding from a number of wounds which resulted in his death. If the shaman's *baohi·'gan* lived in the water his victim met his death by drowning.[2]

A widely known feat among the shamans of northeastern North America is that of appearing to sink knee deep at each step in

---

[1] C. G. Leland, *Algonquin Legends of New England*, p. 342, gives a somewhat similar tale of a hunter's luck being spoiled by a maleficent sorcerer.

[2] Related by Newell Lion to Mr. R. H. Ferris.

either rock, hard earth or ice. Perhaps no other single exploit is so frequently mentioned by writers on the tribes of the region as this one. It occurs in Micmac,[1] Passamaquoddy,[2] and Malecite[3] sources

[1] C. G. Leland, *Algonquin Legends of New England*, Boston, 1885, p. 88, gives an account, apparently Micmac, of how Mikumwess dances "around a circle upon the hard floor. They saw his feet sink deeper at every step and ever deeper as the dances went on; ploughing the ground up into high uneven ridges forming a trench as he went until at length only his head was to be seen."

Another Micmac authority, Stansbury Hagar, "Micmac Magic and Medicine," *Journal of American Folk-Lore*, vol. IX, no. 34 (1896), p. 173, says, "Before a group of his companions a Micmac suddenly giving a terrible shout, danced in a most astonishing way, for at each step he drove his leg into the solid earth up to his knees. The prints of his steps remained until a few years ago in earth on which oxen make no impression, so Abram Glode tells me." Sapiel Sagaman who died about twenty-five years ago at Halifax is said to have been able, when angry enough, to stamp his foot several inches into the rock.

[2] Cf. C. G. Leland (*op. cit.*, p. 341–2). Leland discusses a second hand account of a Passamaquoddy magician who won a bet of ten dollars from some white people, by first screaming so loud that no one could move and then taking "seven steps through the ground up to his ankles as if it had been light snow." Cf. also C. G. Leland, *op. cit.*, p. 291. Leland further says "And very recently in Philadelphia . . . a spiritualist named Gordon performed the very same trick. Having been detected a full account of the manner of action appeared in the press of that city. It was done by a peculiar method of stooping and of concealing the stoop behind a skirt" (p. 342). See also Leland (*op. cit.*, p. 88–89). J. D. Prince, "Some Passamaquoddy Witchcraft Tales," *Proceedings of the American Philosophical Society*, vol. XXXVIII, no. 160 (1900), p. 182, "They (the sorcerers) could violate the laws of nature so far as to walk in hard ground, sinking up to the ankles or knees at every step. He then gives a tale related by Newell S. Francis in the original Passamaquoddy text with a translation as follows (*op. cit.*, p. 185): "When I was fifteen years old, I saw a man who was a wizard. He was called a Mi'kumwess (a wood devil). He told me that he had sunk into hard ground up to his ankles, and he showed me the place where he had done so. I saw the track where he had walked." Cf. also J. D. Prince, "Notes on Passamaquoddy Literature," *Annals of New York Academy of Sciences*, vol. XIII, no. 4 (1901), p. 385. "It was no uncommon feat for *medeolin* to sink up to their knees in hard ground in the presence of a number of people . . . the magician always took seven long steps at each of which he sank up to his knees in the hardest earth." The feat is called *quetkeosag*.

[3] Gabe Paul relates an account of a Malecite shaman supposed to have lived in New Brunswick who once took three steps sinking knee-deep in the solid rock and then sat down. Where he trod and where he lay his bow when he sat down are marked by deep imprints now.

Gabe Perley (a Malecite from Tobique) more definitely ascribed a similar feat to Sapiel Sockalexis a *mǝdéolinu*, who died about thirty years ago. The version states that Sockalexis exposed his power, after a quarrel with his wife, by taking seven steps in a hard-trodden path, each time sinking his boots about four inches into the ground. Perley claims to have seen the marks.

and even among the Greenland Eskimo.[1] In one particular case the feat is also ascribed in a general way to the Penobscot conjurers of the past, the direct testimony which I have gathered being contained in the following passage, from the dictation of Old Joe Francis who died in 1916.

My grandfather was regarded as a *məde'olinu*. Often at night he would make his footprints in the solid rock where everybody could see them in the morning. He worked at night.

Another case occurs in a myth. Here the hero wrestles with an opponent. Each time that he is brought down upon the ground on his feet he sinks up to his knees and becomes stronger at each occasion until he is able to overcome the enemy.[2]

Old Mitchell Francis, a Passamaquoddy whose *baohi''gan* was a wolf, is also accredited with having accomplished this feat at Oldtown, where he lived and died. The tale relates how having been persuaded to try his power (*udagwet'ha'n'dowin*) on one occasion near Bucksport, he made tracks in hard ground, denting the ground as deep as his ankles. Several people living at Oldtown until recently, one of them old Sabattis Shay, believed this account and claimed before me that they had seen the tracks.

A number of short accounts of the doings of the shamans, many of which from the native standpoint might, indeed, just as well be included among the myths, are given here where they seem to bear most directly. It is largely from this class of material, the supply of which seems almost inexhaustible among these Indians, that one has to deduce his general facts. Even the Indians themselves possess no more general means of inquiry into the subject, which I fear is capable of definition now only by means of such brief descriptive narratives.

---

[1] Rink, *Tales and Traditions of the Eskimo*, p. 59.

[2] A very interesting Micmac version of this theme was related to the writer by Joe Toney of the Yarmouth band. In abstract it tells of a war between the Micmac (*Mi'gemawa''tc*) and the western Wabanaki (*Keni' bəwa''tc*). The fighting men would thrust each other into the ground above the ankles. Hence they came to designate the stick which is thrust diagonally into the ground in camp for the suspension of the tea-pot, as *Mi'gemawa''tc* and *Kəni' bewa''tc*, the one by the other. When members of the two tribes are camping together they refrain from referring to the pot-stick lest the reminder awaken the traditional sentiments.

At Bucksport, Maine, where the Indians usually camped the second night in going by canoe down to " salt water ", there is a fine spring of water.   On one occasion they found that a big rock had slid down the bank and choked it up.   The party had to camp without water that night.   But a *məde′olinu* in the party told them that he would make it all right.   The band made camp and went to sleep.   In the morning it was found to be true.   The rock had been removed, although no one had heard it done, and the water was flowing freely again.[1]

A pair of Malecite twins living a generation ago on St. John river were *məde′olinu*.   Among the tricks attributed to them, it was said that one of these boys could hang his hat on a sunbeam, could let people in through locked doors, and could fasten ropes on a burdock plant from which to make a swing for himself.   A good many people had seen these tricks.[2]

There was a boy in the country to the northeast who was *məde′olinu.*   One of the strange things he did was to press a chip of wood against his mother's cheek once when she scolded him.   The chip stuck to her cheek and could not be removed until he himself took it off.

Not long ago a man hereabouts had occasional *məde′olinu* power.   For some reason they sent up to arrest him.   He was camping by a frozen lake when the policeman and a deputy took him.   He said he would submit, but declared that if he wanted to he could slay them both.   While they were crossing over on the ice, he caused it to shake violently though it was several inches thick, and his captors were very much frightened.   They believed that he could do almost anything.   However, he went along with them, though later escaped from the jail.   Another man when he gave himself up to Christianity, forsook his shamanistic powers though it cost him such pangs that he shook and trembled all over and nearly died before his power left him.

All the men of the tribe were afraid of these witch men and did not dare to touch them lest they (the witches) injure them in some way.

The familiar and oft-cited practice of sympathetic action in which injury could be inflicted by shooting the picture or likeness of the intended victim, was known in this region.[3]   Newell Lion relates the belief that, having made an image by outlining in sand

---

[1] The power to lift up and throw a boulder of great size is included in the reputation of a shaman at Yarmouth, N. S., according to a Micmac informant.   A similar feat is attributed to the Malecite shaman previously mentioned.   He is believed to have lifted up and thrown, some distance, a boulder about five feet in diameter.   This heroic feat is also accredited to the transformer Gluskabe.

[2] I have heard of these boys from a number of people.   Gabe Paul furnished this anecdote.

[3] An independent Malecite source, Gabe Perley, gives identical information.

or drawing with a charred stick on bark the figure of his victim, the shaman named it and then shot, stabbed, clubbed or burned the likeness. As a consequence of this action the victim would suffer a corresponding fate unless he could bribe the operator to withdraw the cause or to annul it. It is believed that a small quantity of the victim's hair could be operated upon with the same effect.

Removing disease by suction is a shamanistic feat recorded of the tribes over extensive areas in America. It stands out prominently among the Central Algonkian. Here in the northeast, however, the only indications of such a practice are found in earlier accounts.[1]

Another shaman's trick which I have heard spoken of in the Penobscot village, is that of causing an iron rail to float on water.[2]

The shamans, moreover, often prophesied; for example, the coming of a direful swan was foretold by a shaman, the white creature subsequently becoming identified with the Europeans when they first appeared in ships off the shores of the Penobscot bay. Nicolar tells the story.[3] Prophecy is one of the general characteristics of the ancient shamans.[4] The power of increasing or diminishing his size is another shaman's attribute.[5] Again we hear of others who could even bore a hole in a tree and extract their favorite drink from it, plugging it up when they had drawn enough.[6]

The ability to handle fire, so commonly attributed to shamans

---

[1] Nicholas Denys, "Description and Natural History of the Coasts of North America" (1672), *Edition of the Champlain Society*, p. 417, Toronto, 1908, by W. F. Ganong, and Chrêtienne Leclerq, "New Relation of Gaspesia" (1691), p. 217–223, *ibid.*, 1910, by W. F. Ganong. These authors describe practices of Micmac shamans in some detail, mentioning blowing, and evidently, sucking the seat of pain in case of sickness.

[2] The same is mentioned among the Micmac according to S. Hagar, "Micmac Magic and Medicine," *Journal of American Folk-Lore*, vol. IX, no. 34, p. 173. The Micmac of Nova Scotia also attribute this feat to Sapiel Sagaman, a magician who died about twenty-five years ago. It is claimed that he was seen to make float a stone, axe, and saw.

[3] Joseph Nicolar, pp. 97–105. For a Micmac mention of the power of prophecy, see S. T. Rand, *Legends of the Micmacs*, p. 144, footnote.

[4] The power of prophesying is mentioned explicitly of the ancient Abenaki by A. Maurault, *Histoire des Abenakis*, pp. 29, 30, 122, 125.

[5] Also Micmac (S. T. Rand, *Legends of the Micmacs*, p. 171), "he was a brave boöin having the power of enlarging or diminishing his size at will."

[6] A similar feat is ascribed to a Micmac shaman by Joe Toney.

among the central tribes, seems to be practically unknown to the records of shamanism in the northeast. Extended inquiry failed to disclose knowledge of it except for a couple of cases quite negligible in significance. One of these states that a shaman was known to light his pipe by slowly holding a live coal on the bowl, and to spread the live coals in a fire with the bare hand so that a bean pot could be put there. Both of these performances however could be accomplished by a horny-handed lumberman without much discomfort.

A qualitative feature of the northeastern shaman's magic, not to be overlooked, is that the power had to be conserved lest it give out if drawn upon too much at one time.[1]

The anecdotes concerning Edmund Francis,[2] the *mǝde'olinu* by repute at Oldtown, mentioned before, are as follows: He boasts, or they say that he did once, of being able to cross his legs on a chair and then lift himself from the floor by pulling up on the rungs of the chair. He tells that once he made camp on the banks of a distant stream. When he got ready to leave he started to jump across, the stream being quite wide. Half way over he remembered that he had left behind his axe and in mid-air turned about, grabbed the axe and finished his jump without alighting. Once in camp with Frank Joe, up near the Mattawamkeag, he jumped up in the middle of the night from a deep sleep and fired his gun into the air twice in succession. When questioned about his queer behavior he declared that he wanted to scare away some white folks whom he felt to be approaching. Once when he was working with a gang on a log jam, he slipped off a rolling log and fell under the jam where he lay at the bottom for about three hours: He claimed that he could see the ends of the poles which the men poked down into the water to find him. He heard them saying, "Poor Edmun', he must be drowned by this time, poor fellow!" But he only wanted

---

[1] Commented upon also by W. H. Mechling concerning the Malecite, *Malecite Tales*, p. 4, and by C. G. Leland for the Passamaquoddy, *Algonquin Legends of New England*, p. 221. A rabbit in one tale had come almost to an end of his *m'téoulin* or wizard power for that time, yet he had still enough left for one more great effort," and again, p. 367.

[2] This old man died uneventfully in 1914.

to scare them. He pushed aside the poles and stayed down until he got tired, then jumped up from the water and surprised them all.[1] Another time he became stranded on a rock in the midst of a very swiftly running rapids. He jumped upon what he thought was a log rushing by. It carried him into a log jam, and when it struck he jumped from it and then discovered that it was merely a roll of hollow bark. He thought it was a magic tree.

Upon another occasion Francis claimed to have been able to bend his gunbarrel so that when he fired at a curved line of ducks his bullet took a course that penetrated all the ducks in the line.

THE DREAMER

The second order of magical practitioners is represented by individuals whose power lay in their ability to foresee events, to penetrate in a dream vision the barriers which prevent ordinary human beings from seeing the spiritual forces which underlie acts and which animate various creatures. They were shamans of a humbler sort. A dreamer, as we may call him, was known as *ki'ugwa'sowi''no*[2] "man who searches about in dreams." Our direct information about this class of functionaries, since they are persons of the past, is very meager indeed, and leaves a number of vacant gaps. This makes it difficult to coördinate the social position and functions of the dreamer with what we know of similar personages among the Algonkian north of the St. Lawrence and those of the central group. From several informants, chief among whom Newell Lion again figures, I will now quote the data which have been brought to light, leaving the tentative discussion and comparative treatment until later when we have learned all that there is to know from the Penobscot sources.

The dreamers had the power to go to sleep and, while in this condition, to see what events where going to take place in the future.

---

[1] S. T. Rand, *Legends of the Micmacs*, p. xliii, xliv, mentions the same of the Micmac. The writer's Micmac notes contain reference to the claim that at one of the Wabanaki councils with the Iroquois at Caughnawaga the Micmac delegate swam through the La Chine rapids under water.

Penobscot tradition in general confirms the claim that some shamans could remain for a long time under water. (Informants, Charles Daylight and others.)

[2] *Ki'*- "going about," *-gwaso* dream, *-i'no* "person."

Their duty in this capacity was to warn of danger so that those who received the warning could employ means to ward the trouble off or to avoid it. The power of the dreamer was employed not only for individuals but for the benefit of the community. Before undertaking a hunting trip parties would induce a dreamer to lie down, go to sleep, and "look around" (*gwi·la'wɑbo*).[1] By the nature of the vision which the dreamer had, the party would form its plans or alter them in case plans had been made which appeared unadvantageous from the dreamer's revelation. Dreamers, moreover, were often induced to accompany hunting or war parties in order to serve with their gifts of vision. It was only necessary for the dreamer to spend one night obtaining the answer that he desired. The informants agree that the dreamers were harmless in their behavior towards other men, they never inflicted injury, sickness, or misfortune upon rivals, as we find the *mɔde'olinu* so frequently doing. They, too, were not formed into any society. Since we have very little definite knowledge of the achievements of dreamers we have to rely upon anecdotes which appear, in the opinions of modern narrators, to belong to the category of dreamer accomplishments. For instance, Newell Lion himself cited several occasions upon which he had encountered in dreams the spirit helper (*baohi·'-gan*) of malevolent persons. These visions he thought illustrated in some respects the mental visitations which he understood to have been so extensively relied upon by the ancient dreamers. Taking our information even at its maximum it is plain that here we have only a vestige of what must evidently have been a prominent matter of early Indian life in this region. The anecdotes which fall under this category are as follows:

Newell Lion's wife's uncle once dreamed that he was camping not far from his brother-in-law, to whom he had attributed certain ill-luck. The two did not get along well together. So this season when the hunting had become very bad, the uncle dreamed that a wolf entered the door of his wigwam. In his dream he hit the animal with a stick and it departed. Shortly after this dream a friend from his brother-in-law's camp came to ask him for some

---

[1] *gwi·láo-* "to search for," *-wɑb-* "to see."

medicine for a sick man. It was known that only medicine given by the victor who caused the wound could cure the conquered magician. The uncle then went to his brother-in-law's camp and discovered him suffering with a severe hurt on his shoulder. Said the uncle, "Don't sneak around my camp any more!" He then gave him some medicine which subsequently cured him. If he had not given his brother-in-law the medicine the latter would have died.[1]

Newell Lion's grandmother once dreamed that she saw a dog come into her camp. The dog bit her on the elbow. When she hit the dog it fell over dead. It then presented the appearance of a certain person whom she knew. When she awoke she found that her elbow was sore and it remained so for the rest of her life. The person whose likeness she saw in the dead dog in her dream died shortly after.

Newell Lion himself claims that he dreamed of seeing a bull at the entrance of his shanty. He attacked the bull and threw it over, whereupon he recognized a certain man whom he knew to have been frequently speaking against him in the village. Upon another occasion he dreamed that a big snake attacked him. Taking a stick he struck it on the head. As it fell over and died he recognized one whom he had supposed to be a friend. When he consulted with an older man about the dream he was informed that it was a warning concerning an enemy in disguise.

---

[1] Four years before the above account was given by Newell Lion, Mr. Ferris took down one from him which closely follows mine, except in the last four sentences. It affords us another instance of the extent to which an informant may vary his narrative at different times.

"The uncle, however, procured an ordinary root and cured him with it. He told the man never to match his power against his and the man was glad enough to promise the same, as the uncle had given sufficient proof of his ability as a dreamer."

Mr. Ferris has the following to say in his notes on the same subject.

"The dreamer, however, had but to dream (this dream was generally always of the same type except that the animals varied as to species) of an animal coming into his wigwam or pursuing him in one way or another and to kill this animal with his club when the form of the witch-man would replace that of his "*baohi'gan.*" If the dreamer then wished it he had the power to cure the witchman upon whom he had thrown the fatal spell. As to his own experience Newell Lion spoke of two dreams that he himself had had of animals and both the men into whom they had changed when he attacked them in the dream had been his enemies and had died afterward. He stoutly disclaimed, though, that he was a dreamer."

Attean Orson was a great wrestler.   He was down on the coast
one time hunting seals near the upper end of Mt. Desert island.
He killed quite a few seals and started for home.   He camped at
Hog island coming up the river.   After supper he fell asleep but
was soon awakened by a strange noise.   His tent was knocked
down and dragged away.   He wondered greatly at this because
at the time there was no wind.   Then he rolled up his tent and
put it under his head.   Soon he felt himself grasped by the feet
and he cried: "Who are you?   Show yourself!   Give me fair play!"
He then felt something seize hold of him and he began to wrestle
and kept it up all night.   Towards morning when he had his
enemy down as it became light he saw that he had been wrestling
with an old wind-fall.   Orson said that whenever he hit the spirit
in his fight it would hit him back in the same place.   He always
claimed that this was an experience with someone's *baohi·'gan* and
that he had fought through and conquered.[1]

Lion, to whom this story had been related by the hero himself,
alleged that Orson must have had a nightmare in the first place
and then must have become so frightened that he had fought for
a while with himself.   Orson's interpretation of the event, however,
as an experience with a *baohi·'gan* in the guise of a wind-fall, is
what interests us.[2]

Probably nearly all the modern accounts of *baohi·'gan* deeds
are based upon dream experiences like the last few tales.   And
it may be too that much weight should for this reason be given to
dream experiences as an explanation of the whole fabric of recent
shamanistic lore.

We have another instance of the operation of maleficent magic
through dream action in the following.[3]   Mary Paul, daughter of

[1] Charles Daylight, a Penobscot, also narrates a version of this tale in which the
antagonist, during the night, promised the man unlimited worldly power if he would
stop, but the offer was not accepted.

[2] A remarkably similar anecdote is given by C. G. Leland, *Algonquin Legends of
New England;* Boston, 1884, pp. 348-9, related to him by a Passamaquoddy, Tomah
Josephs.   The hero of the tale fought all night with what he thought was a ghost
which appeared in the form of a moss covered log the next morning.   He acquired
magic power by his contest.

[3] A Malecite incident related by the chief character's brother, G. A. Paul.

Andrew Paul, of Kingsclear, New Brunswick, received a proposal of marriage accompanied by the wampum message from a young man whom she refused. Soon afterward becoming afflicted with sore throat she laid the blame upon the disappointed man. Subsequently her father dreamed that this man entered his camp, upon which he seized a stick and struck him with it. A few days after it was learned that this man had received a hurt in the head. The incidents governed by the native concept in such a case became associated in the minds of those concerned and the two families became unfriendly.

The neighboring tribes (Micmac,[1] Malecite, Passamaquoddy,[2] Abenaki[3]) as may be expected, seem to show similar characteristics

[1] Leclercq (1691) says of the Micmac "Our Gaspesians are still so credulous about dreams that they yield easily to everything which their imagination or the Devil puts into their heads when sleeping and this is so much the case among them that dreams will make them come to conclusions upon a given subject quite contrary to those which they had earlier formed. Chr. Leclercq, "New Relation of Gaspesia," *Edition of the Champlain Society*, Toronto, 1910, by W. F. Ganong, p. 227. Also (*ibid.*, p. 216), "They imagine also that their jugglers can know from their Devil whom they call *Ouahich* (possibly *waitci'tc* "little beast" meaning an animal helper) the best places for hunting, and that all the dreams of these imposters are just so many revelations and prophecies." . . . and again, on page 223, "Some of these jugglers also meddle with predictions of future affairs and in such a way that if their predictions are found correct, as happens sometimes by chance, they derive credit and reputation from this fact." S. T. Rand, *Legends of the Micmacs*, Boston, 1881, p. 139, narrates a tale of how a hunter dreams of trouble at home and returns to find that the Mohawks have attacked his family.

The Micmac employ two terms to designate the dreamer, *ne'bɔdi'deuk*, "clairvoyant," and *nudji'bu''wat* "dreamer."

[2] Cf. C. G. Leland, *Algonquin Legends of New England*, Boston, 1884, pp. 343–5, where a talk is given in which a young man wished to acquire this power of dreaming for luck. He was told to test himself by living in abstinence for a while with a virgin. He did so and acquired the power to divine all things by dreams when he slept on a magic bear's skin. He could tell where to find good hunting and fishing. He foredreamed war with the Mohawk. Stones in the forest are thought to give power to dream. One informant claimed to have dreamed that he saw magicians dive under the water from one island to another (p. 345). (Malecite, *ki'u'kwa'sowi''no.*)

[3] Cf. Abbè Maurault, *Histoire des Abenakis*, Quebec, 1866, p. 122. "They had jugglers who could foretell good or bad fortune by messages from the spirits . . .," *ibid.*, p. 125. "The shamans had a way of predicting that such or such a person or party would have bad fortune by falling into the hands of the Iroquois. Thus they won their prestige as prophets," *ibid.*, p. 29. Conjurers had the "power to predict good and bad weather, good or bad fortune in hunting, the mishaps which will happen on a journey, the result of a campaign and a thousand other things."

in respect to the dreamers as those which stand forth among the Penobscot. The accounts of dream functionaries in earlier literary sources fall in well with what we learn from modern informants on the subject, as may be seen. The older authorities do not contain much that is not obtainable even today, while in what they do give there is nothing contradictory to the modern material.

The absence of organization as an artificial social unit is a noteworthy feature here and the same is true of the Naskapi and Montagnais, while in the provinces of the Central Algonkian and on the Plains the dreamers seem to have constituted groups of ceremonialists. The situation in the far east in respect to the dreamers resembles that already discussed in the case of the shamans. This is true of the tribes both north and south of the St. Lawrence. For instance, among the Naskapi[1] and the Montagnais, who are the most remote from the area where organized ceremonial groups prevail, the dreamers and shamans are purely individualists. The eastern Cree[2] seems to be the first group, passing toward the west, where the graded society of shamans of the Midewin type occurs.

THE OLDER ALGONKIAN SHAMANISM

Concerning shamanism in the northeast, no striking cases of similarity either in name or in function have been recorded among the Algonkian tribes outside of the immediate area of the related group. The form content of the various types of magical practice, while it is fairly uniform throughout the whole Algonkian area seems to have its parts distributed rather unequally among the different tribes. In the east, among the Wabanaki, the magicians do not form the constituents of a society group, as is the

[1] "They are also guided to a great extent by their dreams, for they imagine that in the night they are in direct communications with the spirits which watch over their daily occupations. Certain persons obtain much renown in divining the dreams and these are consulted with the greatest confidence. The drum is brought into use, and during its tumult the person passes into a state of stupor or trance and in a few moments arouses himself to reveal the meaning of the other's dream. L. M. Turner, "Ethnology of the Ungava District," *Eleventh Annual Report, Bureau of American Ethnology,* Washington, p. 272.

[2] Cf. A. B. Skinner, "Notes on the Eastern Cree and Northern Saulteaux," *Anthropological Papers, American Museum of Natural History,* vol. IX, part I (1911), p. 63, 67, for dream functions.

case among the central tribes. In the east there are only two orders of magicians, in the central area there are from three (Ojibwa) to six (Menomini[1]). In the east the magician of the one kind performs jugglery, inflicts injury, removes injury, cures illness, fights rivals and operates to carry out his arbitrary intentions through the aid of an animal spirit helper. In the central region these activities are divided among different kinds of performers who are ordinarily organized into separate societies, and then in addition the functions of the animal helpers are much specialized or limited. In short, as respects shamanism, the eastern tribes show a lack of socialization, a lack of specialization in function.

Although the present state of disorganization may be due to culture degeneracy it seems nevertheless to be a rather genuine quality of the ethnology of the region, because we do not encounter mention of more elaborate ceremonies in the early records. It should be remembered also that our informants' knowledge dates back about 60 years to a period when native life was much more intact.

The supposition that we have an old Algonkian feature in the individualistic character of shamanism in the north and northeast is in harmony with the explanation, given by Dr. Wissler, of certain circumstances in connection with the shamanistic cults of the Plains area. Here, among the Algonkian tribes of the Plains, the cult-like associations of shamanism are "conspicuously absent, shamanism being less intense and entirely individualistic."[2] In the Plains area the cult-like organizations are shown by Wissler and Lowie to be probable diffusions from a culture-trait center which have reached the more remote tribes only in part, or in some cases not at all. Subsequent study may show that a similar relationship exists between the Central Algonkian, on the one hand and the northern and northeastern branches of the stock on the other as respects shamanistic cults. The central tribes possess an

---

[1] Cf. A. B. Skinner, "Associations and Ceremonies of the Menomini Indians," Anthropological Papers of the American Museum of Natural History, vol. XIII, part II (1915).

[2] Cf. Clark Wissler, "Societies of the Plains Indians," Anthropological Papers of the American Museum of Natural History, vol. XI (1916), p. 858.

organization (Midewin) which has evidently developed from the cohesion of diffused culture elements. Yet outside of and dis-associated from this organization two professional classes of shamans (Wabanu and Djesakid) occur in practically all the tribes of the group.[1] In such a case we might form an idea, in an attempt at explanation, that shamanism was originally individualistic in char-acter among the old Algonkian, at a time prior to the appearance of the Midewin as an organization.

It would be a mistake to overlook the opportunity at this time of making a few comparisons between shamanism in this region and the practices in the better-known surrounding culture areas. The northeastern Algonkian material is noticeably disparate from Iroquois shamanistic practices, so we are left to compare its elements, treating the whole northeast as an areal unit, with the practices of the Central Algonkian on the one hand and the Eskimo on the north. The correspondences with Central Algonkian shamanism are indeed no more striking than are those with Eskimo shamanism, which unavoidably means something in the latter case. In the first place the shamanistic societies of the central region are lacking in the northeast, as they are also among the Eskimo. Shamans operate less with magic paraphernalia and more with animal spirit helpers among both the northeastern tribes and the Eskimo than among the central tribes where "medicine-bundle" influence seems to be strong. Aside from negativism there are some positive analogues in shamanistic tricks among the northeastern tribes and the Eskimo. Surveying, for instance, the conjurer's performances

---

[1] A. B. Skinner, "Political and Ceremonial Organization of the Plains Ojibway," *ibid.*, p. 505, and "Associations and Societies of the Menomini Indians," *ibid.*, vol. XIII (1915), p. 191, and "A Comparative Sketch of the Menomini," *American Anthro-pologist*, N. S., vol. XIII (1911), no. 4, p. 561, and particularly Wm. Jones, "The Central Algonkin," *Annual Archeological Report of Ontario* (1905), pp. 135, 146. There is considerable significance in this connection with Dr. Radin's interpretative analysis of Midewin initiation ceremonies among the central tribes. "It is evidently a formal transfer of shamanistic powers from one individual to another, which has subsequently become synonymous with admission into the social status of a mide and then with admission into a society." Cf. Paul Radin, "The Ritual and Significance of the Winne-bago Medicine Dance," *Journal of American Folk-Lore*, vol. XXIV, no. XCII (1911), p. 186. Shamanistic individualism is associated with the absence of ritualism, as a feature of primitiveness by Clark Wissler, *The American Indian*, 1917, p. 188-9.

of this region, a noticeable portion are recorded in similar form by various authors dealing with the Eskimo. The following are a few; stamping feet into ice or stone, lifting a heavy rock, rendering one's self invisible, causing a heavy object to float, remaining under water, fatal pointing with the finger, diminishing one's size, miraculous wrestling, foretelling the future, and other less striking parallels.

Eskimo angakok tricks not occurring among the northeastern tribes are, the changing of sex, tearing the skin from the face, submitting to decapitation and burning, and divination by head lifting.

Turning from the northeast toward the central area the following features are common to both, shaman fights by proxy, prophesying through visions and dreams, the overpowering voice, and some others, while the fire trick and the sword swallowing trick common in the central area do not occur in the northeast.

There are three possible ways of explaining these Eskimo-Algonkian correspondences.[1] (1) The features could have been acquired by borrowing from the Eskimo if we assume Algonkian invaders to have experienced a period of contact with earlier Eskimo inhabitants. (2) The features could have been independently conceived by the two groups, the similarities resulting from convergent steps in their development. (3) They could have been borrowed by the Eskimo from the Indians. The two latter possibilities in this case are hardly to be considered probable. The first, however, appeals much more to reason. The analogous tricks are widely known among the Eskimo, even among those of Greenland who have had no direct contact with Indians, and consequently may have constituted old Eskimo property. In general, assuming the Indians to have killed off the Eskimo, if there were any on the Canadian maritime coast, at some early time, the relics of their culture could only have persisted among the surviving Indians and their descendants.

Although much more detailed material is awaited concerning

---

[1] Incidentally it may be noted that significant ethnological similarities are by no means restricted to shamanism when alone Eskimo and northeastern Indian culture are compared.

the tribes north of the St. Lawrence as well as the others of the Wabanaki group it seems to me that almost enough has already been accumulated and presented to show that the circumstances here of simplicity and the individualistic character of shamanism are real qualities in the ethnology of this region.

Corresponding simplicity and individualism together character-ize the institution of shamanism among the tribes north of the St. Lawrence. Thus both these extreme eastern regions, which are equally remote from contact with the more complex and more ceremonialized Central Algonkian tribes, we find to be noteworthy for the same elementary simplicity and lack of organization. There are two ways in which the contrast between the northeastern and the central phases of culture may be looked at. On the other hand assuming a process of degeneration to account for present states, we may attempt to trace the eastern conditions backward to a former more elaborate stage comparable perhaps to that which flourished among the tribes of the central group. Let us briefly review this possibility. There is something to favor such an assumption in the facts of history and geographical association, for we know through local tradition that the Montagnais and Naskapi are immigrants from the west to the northeast[1] and we have reason to credit a similar Wabanaki claim that their prede-cessors came from farther west. Thus there appears to have been a two-fold, possibly a bifurcated drift, down the St. Lawrence basin from the central regions, one stream penetrating the country north of its shores, and the other covering the region of its southern water-shed to the ocean. The culture gradations among the Algon-kian from the Atlantic coast on the east to the central lake region may be explained if one choose to do so, by assuming a process of deculturation as migration proceeded from the central region east-ward toward the north Atlantic coast.

There is, however, still the other attitude toward the situation; one that accepts the evidence of simplicity in culture as natural,

---

[1] Such a tradition is current among the Montagnais generally and it is confirmed by the testimony recorded in the *Jesuit Relations* which deal with the tribes of eastern Quebec

representative of a more elementary type. In this case we would interpret conditions here by inferring that the eastern tribes have retained a form of simple primitive culture which the central tribes have outgrown, or perhaps which the latter have lost through the acquisition of a higher, more formal one resulting from contact with superior culture forces. The likelihood of the eastern emigration of the Algonkian does not pose as a strong objection in this case because such a migration at an early time would have served to remove part of the primitive Algonkian group from the range of outside culture influence and left this body as the conserver of simple culture by reason of its self-isolation. In this case, going from east to west, we should expect to find the culture gradations just spoken of and besides this a certain local individuality in customs due to the irregularity of tribal developments when they are progressing from a simple nascent stage through the various periods of growth congenial to their circumstances. We do find these variations in many minor respects of culture, from tribe to tribe in the group, so much so in some ethnological topics that the differences would be natural to tribes which are widely separated instead of to neighbors as is the case in some respects among the Penobscot, Malecite, and Micmac.

Local variations are considerably less in the Montagnais-Naskapi group north of the St. Lawrence, the more marked uniformity here being plausibly an evidence of a more recent dispersion from the earlier culture center. There is ample historical ground for this idea because within historic times the Montagnais have expelled the Eskimo from the St. Lawrence coast and have themselves been pressed upon by the Iroquois. The Wabanaki group on the other hand has been resident where we find it located for some time prior to the opening of the historical period since we have no records here of extensive tribal movements. Hence, it would seem, these bodies have had a longer period of stability in which to develop local minor differences.

On the whole the second possibility appeals more strongly to my mind as a means of explanation than the first. In this case simplicity, lack of complex social, religious and ceremonial organization, limited nomadism, subsistence by hunting and fishing, no agriculture and a crude technology, are together the earmarks of a relatively unaffected older Algonkian type of culture. In the neighboring Eskimo region a somewhat similar situation prevails, as is shown by Dr. Boas. The Central Eskimo are more primitive, more isolated and simpler in culture than those of Alaska whose advancement in social ceremonial and industrial complexity is partially due to contact with the organized culture of the Northwest Coast tribes. As applied to human culture, moreover, the assumption that progressive growth from the simple to the complex is more natural and normal than retrogression, logically requires less proof than the opposite, making proper allowances, to be sure, for historical fluctuations.

TEXTS OF SOME SHAMANISTIC TALES IN THE WABANAKI DIALECTS

The following tales in several of the original dialects will convey a proper idea of the character of the specific narrative dealing with the deeds of shamans. They have been selected from the writer's collections of mythological texts in the dialects of the northeast. Several tales recorded in English are also added.

The system of transcription used is that recommended by the Committee of the American Anthropological Association, *Smithsonian Miscellaneous Publications*, vol. 66, pp. 120–6 (1916).

PHONETIC NOTE

    a, as in *father*, of medium length.

    a·, lengthened.

    e, open medium about as *e* in *met*. In Wawenock this sound is still more open, approaching the next vowel (ϵ·) in value.

    ϵ·, long open *e*, as in North German *Bär*.

    e·, close and long as *a* in *say*.

    i, short as in *pin*.

    i·, long and close as *ee* in *queen*.

    o, close, medium in length.

    ɔ·, close and longer with more protruding lips.

    u, like *oo* in *boot*.

    u·, long with protruded lips.

    α, dulled form of short *a*, like *u* of English *but*.

e, short obscure vowel of uncertain quality like *e* in *flower*.

b-p, bilabial stops.

d-t, alvoelar stops, no lingual-dental contact.

g-k, medial palatal stops.

s-z, dorsal sibilants.

} Varying between true sonant and intermediate surd-sonant.

tc and *dj*, surd and sonant affricatives correspond in Penobscot respectively to English *ch* and *j*. In St. Francis Abenaki these sounds are like English *ts* and *dz*.

m, as in English.

n,

η, palatal nasal like *ng* of English *sing*.

l, as in English.

ł, crossed *l*, soft lateral surd, tongue tip and alveolar contact, preceded and accompanied by aspiration. The effect of this sound is approximated by condensing vowel followed by aspiration and *l*; (*i'la*).

h,

w, } as in English.

y,

ą, *ǫ*, *ą̣*, nasalized vowel.

ʻ, aspiration following vowel or consonant.

ʼ, accent stress, ˋ secondary accent.

˙, a dot following denotes vowel or consonant lengthening.

1. *The Trial-Contest Meetings of the Magicians* (Penobscot)

Boʼskiˑnąwat	*məde'oliˑnawak*	*nąˑʼdjiˑ*	*agwetʻhan˙do'ldowak*
Occasionally long ago	magicians	went	trying their magic power

nəgwa'zəbemuk   *piˑgwa'duk*   *tandj udliˑʼgiˑziˑ   waniˑhalzo'ldiˑną*
to the lake.   "Abundance of Game"[1] how   at last could they disappear and escape

kmipʻhagwɑ'loden   *ao'diˑmge*   *kadiˑseʻka'wode*   *ne'dudjiˑ*   *a'eda*
if they were pursued   in war   about to be defeated.   So then   a'eda

nɑ'nɑgwutc   kamgwiˑʼgədaho   tcawaʻpiˑʼgədaho   mu'skiˑde   eliˑgiˑʼziˑ
some   dove into the water jumped into the water emerging   how could

kwulbiˑha'lzu   kiˑʼuniˑge   ntciˑgəda'k   ukamgwiˑʼgədahin   muskte'siˑge
change himself into   otter   and others   dove into the water when emerging

aliˑgwulbiˑha'lzu   məde'wiˑle ntciˑgəda'k ukamgwiˑʼgədahin muskte'siˑge
how change himself into   loon   and others dove into the water when emerging

eliˑgiˑziˑgwulbiˑha'lzu   muskweʼʼsˑu ntciˑgəda'k   eliˑgiˑziˑgwulbiˑha'lzu
how could change himself into   muskrat   and others how could change himself into

təmaʼʼkwe ntciˑgəda'k ukamgwiˑʼgədahin muskte'siˑge   eliˑgwulbiˑha'lzu
beaver   and others   dove into the water when emerging how change himself into

---

[1] Now known as Pushaw Lake.

mu'zebe's·u·   *uli·dəhazo'ldowak*   *eli·gi·'zi·*   *təbi·'notlə'di·hi·dit*   *el·han·-*
mink.   They rejoiced   how could they display [to each other]   such
dol'di·hi·dit.
they perform magic.

✸ *Free Translation*

Occasionally long ago the shamans were accustomed to go to
Pushaw (Pi·gwa'duk) Lake to test their magic power. One of
their performances was to cause themselves to disappear as they
would do if they were defeated by an enemy and forced to escape
by flight. Some of them would indeed, dive into the water and
emerge after having been transformed into otters, others into loons,
muskrats, beavers, and minks. They rejoiced in being thus able
to display to each other how they could perform magic acts.

2. *Two Spies Change Themselves into Animals and Escape from the Iroquois* (Penobscot)

Nạwa't   *ni·'zwak*   *ski·no·'sak*   *nadawəhewi·'n·owak*   *ta'gwi·t·e*
Long ago   two   young men   spy men   both indeed

ktahɑ'n·dowak   *unạ'dji·*   *unada'uhạna*   *Megwai*   *wa'kạ'lozən*   *məzi·'*
great magicians   went   [to] they spy into Iroquois   stockade   all

ugi·'zi·   *nadauhạda'mənɑ*   *wedji·'tc*   *gi·zi·'*   *se'kawa'dit*   *me'gwa'*
they could   they investigated   so that   could   they defeat   the Iroquois.

nonadəgwa·'si·nạ   *edali mɑgwạ'gwek skamo'ni·bagwul nogəzạdegwa·'si·nạ*
Then they went to sleep where   on a heap   corn husks   then they overslept.

ma'lam sạŋkhi·'le gi·'zo's sala·'ki·   *mɑskwa'lạmit me'gwe nodo'ki·'mgwonạ*
Then   rose   the sun suddenly   whooping   Iroquois, they they awoke

nodạme'ke'gəda'hi·nạ   *uda'dəbi·gwe'nsi·nạ*   *mala'm ki·'zi·*   *ạŋgawi·ha'zowak*
and jumped up   they rolled themselves   Then   after they were out of sight
                            down out of sight.

nogwulbi·ha'lzi·nạ   *awe·'sus*   *pe'sego*   *kəda'k*   *tci·ma'lsəm*   *ma'ni·*
then they transformed   bear   one man   the other   panther   thereupon
themselves into   a "big wolf"[1]

ogwil·da'wona   *me'gwal*   *gi·ze'lmipho'weli·t*   *odji·*   *mɑndje'kạwa'di·nạ*
they rushed upon the Iroquois after running away   from   they left

ke'nuk məsi·'   *ugi·zạ'bada'mənạ*   *elalok'ha'di·mɑk*   *tane'dudji·*   *gwi·lda'-*
but   all   they had looked it over   what they would do   whenever   they would

mohodit   *wa'kạ'lozən.*
charge upon the stockade.

Free Translation

Long ago there were two young men who acted as spies. Both
were indeed great magicians. They went to spy about an Iroquois
stockade so that they could overcome the Iroquois. After having

---

[1] The ordinary term for panther is *bi·'tɑ'lu* "long tail."   The animal is now unknown to these tribes except by hearsay.

done what they intended they went to sleep upon a pile of corn husks, and they overslept. When the sun arose suddenly the Iroquois began whooping and the young men awoke, jumped up and rolled themselves down the other side out of sight. Being thereupon out of sight of the enemy they transformed themselves, one into a bear, the other into a panther. The Iroquois then rushed upon them but they had run away. To be sure they left the place but they had looked it all over and they knew what could best be done when it was time to attack the stockade.

3. *A Magicians' Contest at Neseik* (Penobscot)

Nọwa't	ni·'zwak	ktci·mɔde'olinowak	udao'di·nα	pe'sɔgo	ali·'wizo.
Long ago	two	great magicians	they fought	one	was called

ktci·asọ's	Nep'tαn[1]	kɔda'k	Plansi·s	Sosep	Nep'tαn	udawe'kαhọ'nα
Big John	Neptune	the other	Francis	Joseph	Neptune	they employed

ubaohi·ga'nu	nɔgwa'zɔbemuk	udali·pɔna'ldi·nọ	nɔgwa'zɔbemuk
their spirit helpers.	In a lake	there they fought	in the lake.

ktci·nahα'mu	naga	ktci·	wi·wi·'lyamek'ʷ	edudji·	sa·'gi·pɔna`ldi·hi·dit
Big eel	and	big	snail	so	hard they fought

e'bɔgwa'tc	nɔgwa'zɔbem	mɔzi·'	unɔs·e'po'dunọ	e'skwat·e	ni·''kwup'
on account of it	the lake	all	they riled up	even yet	now

nse·'gɔn	nαnɔgwa'zɔbem	e'bɔgwa'tc	ni·''kwup'	ali·wi·''tọzu
it is riley	that lake	on account of it	now	it is so called

ne·''segɔk.[2]
Riley [Lake].

The informant added that this fight was a draw; Old John Neptune was a familiar character at Oldtown for many years.

Free Translation

Long ago two great shamans engaged in a fight. One was named Big John Neptune, the other Francis. Joseph Neptune. They both employed their spiritual helpers. They fought in a lake the (spiritual helpers) big eel and the big snail. They fought so hard that on account of it the lake became all riled up and even to this day that lake is still riley and for this reason is called "Riley Lake."

Another version of this same story was obtained by Mr. Ferris from Newell Lion in 1914 while he was in Philadelphia. As duplicate versions of tales told by the same person at different times

---

[1] This man was a Penobscot, his antagonist a Passamaquoddy.

[2] The lake is now known by its Passamaquoddy cognate *Ne·'se·ik* " riley [lake]."

are interesting as specimens of variation in oral literature, the following is given as it appears in Mr. Ferris' notes.

There was much rivalry between the witch men as to whose *baohi''gan* was the strongest. One time a Passamaquoddy Indian said to John Neptune that he had a *baohi''gan*, an immense horned snail as large as a mountain, and he challenged John Neptune's eel to fight it. The contest was arranged and took place in the lake where the eel lived. It was fast and furious and the eel finally proved himself the victor. To this day the lake is muddy particularly when the wind blows and churns up its waters.

A Passamaquoddy version, giving the tale from another point of view, is furnished by C. G. Leland (*Algonquin Legends of New England*, pp. 346–7). Old John Neptune (whom Leland mentions under the initials J. N.) goes out to fight a snail. The incidents given are different from those which we have. The disturbance of the lake is an incident in this version. J. D. Prince (*Proceedings, American Philosophical Society* (1899), no. 160, p. 184), records in text a short Passamaquoddy cognate, in which the elements are again different.

Old Joe Benoit, the wizard, changed himself into a big turtle. He had quarreled with another man. The latter changed himself into a great serpent. The wizards fought together at Nēsēyik. After the fighting, the lake was all stirred up.

4. *wda'psak*,[1] Skull Place (St. Francis Abenaki)

sala''ki·wi·	*oba'yana*	*pi'lwi·*	*Magwa'k²*	*oba'yana*	*wa'dji·*	*nandji·'*
Once	there came	strange	Mohawks	came	for	the purpose

mata·n'di·t	*wɔ·ba'nakia'.*	*ma'ɔwi.*	*ki·ni·ma'khadi·ñ*	*na'gwa ba'zugu*
of killing	Abenaki.	At that time [there was] a great dance		one

ma'gwa	*gu'tmaŋgi·da'mą*	*wɔ·ba'nakia''.*	*nagwa·*	*awa'dji·*	*a'ndokawant*
Mohawk	felt pity	for the Abenaki	and	so	he told

a'lnombai	*phanamu'*	*wa'dji·*	*bu'lowadi·t*	*ale''*	*a'gwa*	*sa'kwoza`di·t*
an Indian	woman	to	run away	when	ever	they appeared

ma'gwak.	*na'gwa naodji·'*	*anda'*	*wu·''lumawalmo`ną ni·'nda bu·'lwaoną`*
the Mohawks.	And despite this	not	believe her these not would ran away

yu·'gik msi·''wi· nda bu'lwakwi·k madji'nłaną.	*na'gwa mst·'wi u'dna`mi·na*
these all not ran away were killed.	And all took

ki`naŋgana'	*ni·u'bi·kagna'ktona*	*si·bu·'si·za'k*	*wadji·*	*wski·du·'sa·di·t*
cradle boards	they laid them	in the little creek	so that	they could cross over.

---

[1] Narrated by Maude Benedict at Lake George, New York, 1907. This is the name of an island in the St. Lawrence river near Montreal where the story is believed to have actually occurred. For another version cf. C. G. Leland and J. D. Prince, *Kuloskap The Master*, pp. 244–9.

[2] Said to refer to the eastern Mohawks, *i. e.*, those of Caughnawaga.

nagodji'' ni·u·'mandji·'na ma'gwak madji'nlandi·'t wɔ·ba'nakia'.   na'go
After this   they went away, the Mohawks,   having killed   the Abenaki.   Then

wikwusa'na wda'psak ni·ni·' udusuku·'miną.   na'gwa o'mbadi·ale·di·t
they camped at Skull Place there they   camped for the   And then   returned from the
night.   hunt

wɔ·ba'nakia·k ni·lo·'na·   ga's·i·ŋlomak uda'dalno·mbamų.   nago'dji·
the Abenakis   they were told   how many were killed   of their people.   Thereupon

ulondji'di·t wa'dji· nusuka'wandi·t magwa'.   nagoda'yin ba'zugu
they prepared   to   follow   the Mohawks.   And there was certain one

mdau'linu·¹ nagwa'na gwi·la'ombiŋ wa'dji· wawa'ldamondi·t do'ni
shaman   and he   sought (by conjuring)   to   know   where

wikusa'di·t magwa'k.   nago mdau'linu· unami·a'n alemsiwi·' kawal-
camped   the Mohawks.   And   the shaman   saw   how (they) all   were

di·di·'t na'gwo odjä'gama pka'gant ni·wa'dji· la'mbasa·k msi·'wi·
sleeping   and   he went out   across   so as to   cut open   all

wigwa'olal nagwozi·bi'wi· gada'gik wɔ·ba'nakia·k pka'gɔ di·t a'ni·
their bark canoes.   And thereupon   the others   Abenaki   crossed   over   there

ma'tci· msi·'wi· lo·'na i'li·gawi·di·da·p ma'gwak.   na'gwa i·biwi·
killed   all   (killed) them   as they were sleeping   the Mohawks.   And   only

ba'zagowa· nugudji·ta'ną magwa' nágwani· gadji· ta'wagwa·zaną.
one   they spared   a Mohawk.   And then   off   they·cut his ears.

ni·udji'ni·' di·la'na wa'dji· mandji·'t ni·udandji·mi·'ŋ ale'msiwi·
After this   they told him   to   go away   and tell abroad   how all

mada'mak udalno'mbama'.
had been put   his people.
an end to

Free Translation²

Once upon a time strange Mohawk came for the purpose of
killing the Abenaki. A great dance was going on at the time.
One of the Mohawk took pity on the Abenaki and he told an
Abenaki woman about it and warned her to run away when the
Mohawk appeared. Despite this warning the other Abenaki would

---

¹ Among other things, the conjuror was able to transfer himself from one place to
another in the guise of an animal which served him as a guardian and helper.

² Another Abenaki (St. Francis) version is given by J. D. Prince (*Kuloskap, The
Master*, by C. G. Leland and J. D. Prince, p. 244). Here the scout assumes the
guise of a beaver; the rest of the tale corresponds very closely to the above.

There may be some historical foundation for this legend. A. Maurault records
an event, in the war between the Abenaki and the Iroquois, which took place about
1695. (Cf. A. Maurault, *op. cit.*, pp. 201 and 230.) He records that a war party of
Mohawk camped on an island in Lake Champlain. They were discovered by some
Abenaki whose scout (shaman?) cut their canoes. The Iroquois were then attacked
and killed. It happened that the Iroquois had been cooking a bull's head over their
fire so the place was named "*Otepsek* island of the head" (A. Maurault, p. 231).
Maurault thinks that Charlevoix must have known the tale for he has the island
marked on his map of Lake Champlain as "d'ile aux têtes."

not believe her when she told them and would not run away. All
those who did not were accordingly killed. The Mohawk took
all their cradle-boards and laid them in the bed of a little creek so
that they could cross over. Then after having killed the Abenaki
the Mohawk departed. They lodged that night at "Skull Place"
where they camped. Later when the rest of the Abenaki returned
from the hunt they were told how that many of their people had
been killed. They at once prepared to follow the Mohawk.
Among them was a certain shaman and he conjured and learned
where the Mohawk had camped. The shaman also saw how they
all were sleeping and he went across to where they were and cut
open all their bark canoes. Thereupon the other Abenaki crossed
over and killed all the Mohawk while they were sleeping. Only
one Mohawk was spared. They cut off his ears and told him to go
forth and tell abroad how all his people had been put to death.

5. *How Sorcerers Originated Wampum* (Wawenock)[1]

*Tanł awe'i· aida' dane'dudji bodawa'zi·mɑk' ni·nawa' utai·nɑ' mɑde'-
oli·nowa`k ni·dɑni·'' ekwɑmpsa·'nɑhi·di·'ł' yu'gik mɑdeolinowa'k.   ni·uda'li
wewetɑ'n aweni·'' mliksani·da' ni·gizi·'' bodawazi·mɑ'k ni·ubɑs·kwɑ-
etɑmɑnɑ' ni·udɑm·hadi'n ni·wa' ktci·mɑdeolinu' gesta' pkwudetɑmɑ'nt
ni·wɔ·bɑ'bi. so'gahazo` wudji·'' wudonɑ'k wɔ·bi·gɑ'k ni·wa' mɑdeolinu'
tebɑbwi·wi.' edutsani.'t niwɔ·bɑbi'm ebas·i·wi·'' wɔ·bi·gɔ·n si·bi·wi·''
ebas·i·wi·'' elwemkwi·gɔ'n ni·wa' nodas·ani't mɑdeolinu' nelɑwe' mkazewi·gɔ'n
wɔ·bɑbi'n ni·nawa' yugi·'k mɑdeolinowa'k tanyu'gɔdji· sekɔ·si·dji`k
ni·gi·gɔdji·'' peme'ltodetci·` wɔ·bɑbi' ki·zi·wɔdɑ'mhadi·hi·di·da mɑde'oli-
nowak ni·tɑławe'i· kadawi·'' wɔlɔs·tɑ wɑ'di·hi·di·de` yugi'k ni·zɔk·ani·'gɔso-
wa`k ni·wɔ tambenkek·tona' wɔ·bɑbi·'' ni·l·ɑ'mpskahɑzu` kɔdɔgwabi·zu'n
ni·dalɑ'mpskɔhɑzu' ni·zno'l wɔldji·a'l· eli·danławei·'' gi·zi·'' wɔlɔ's·tawɑdɔ-
hidi·`t nda'tɑma mɑdɑbe'k`ᵂ nda'tci· gadona'ldi·wi·a`k ni·askami·wi·''
ni·a'tci· nimsi· wi·'.*

Literal Translation

Accordingly whenever a council was held, sorcerers were there.
And according to the strength of their power, it could be known
which were the most powerful. After the council was finished they
lighted pipes, and they all smoked. Then the greatest sorcerer
among them, every time he would light his pipe, would cause

[1] Narrated at Becancour, P. Q., by Francois Neptune, 1913.

wampum to fall from his mouth. The most powerful produced white, he of middling power his wampum was half white and half reddish, and the least powerful sorcerer, his wampum was almost black.[1] So then among these sorcerers he would be the winner who among them would have produced the most wampum when he smoked his pipe. Accordingly whenever two nations wanted to make a treaty they gave as a payment, the beads worked into a belt with two hands embroidered on it, meaning that they had agreed to no more war and that forever they would never hunt one another again. And that is all.

A Shaman Discovered in Bird Form (Penobscot)

Be′zəgwəda   ni·′zwi·ek   us·agi·′a‵kwamalsu   ni·be′bi·′tawan
Once   my wife   became very sick.   I sat up with her

nəbedji·ga′duksin   nəge′wi·a   elgwa′′si·a   ki·′′   sala′′kit′e   mat′gami·gi·′′pode
then I fell asleep.   While I slept   dreaming   ki.‵   suddenly   ground heaved

ma′n·aba   təgu′   pạb′mi·′   wi·′wuni·lạ‵de   eda′li·   a′′kwama′lsit
like   wave   moving up and down   going around.   Where the sick one [lay]

ni·′zwi·ek   nelạbi·a′′   si·′′psi·s   pebami·′dəwi·′′lat   alamka′mi·gwe   ndi·′′lan
my wife   then I looked   bird   flying up and down   under ground.   I said

e‵kwi·gạ′lzi·   kəna′mi·hul   gi·s   moski·a′zi   gi·s   kəna′mi·hul   ki·a
"don′t hide yourself   I see you   already"   he emerged   "already   I see you   you

nela′lo‵kan   we′dji·   a‵kwα′malsit   ni·′zwi·ek‵   en·ekwạbədo′nka   nəb‵mi·′
doing this   so that   she is sick   my wife."   As I said this   moving up and down

moski·′′posi   nna′ste   ume′′tci·na   nəndo′′ki·hazin   to‵ki·′la   mewi·ama′lsu
he emerged;   soon   he died   then I felt   When awake   felt better
                                               myself to waken.

ni·′zwi·ek‵   ne′bəgwa   uga·′win   na′t′e   askα′mat   we′lαyusit.
my wife   on account of it   she slept   at once   entirely   she recovered.

Free Translation

Once when my wife was sick, I sat up with her and soon fell asleep. While sleeping I dreamed that the ground suddenly began to heave like a wave, rising and falling round and round near where the sick one, my wife, lay. Then I saw the movement of a bird[2] flying about under the ground and I said, "Don't hide yourself, I have seen you." The bird emerged. "I have seen you already.

---

[1] Some old woman would come and catch it in her lap when it fell from the sorcerers' mouths.

[2] The informant said that this was a red bird, possibly the scarlet tanager (*Piranga erythromelas*).

You were doing this while my wife was sick." As I said this fluttering he (the bird) came out and died. Then I woke up. When I awoke my wife felt better and fell asleep right away. She got completely well.

The Shaman in Spider Form (Penobscot)

Be'səgwəda   *ge'wi·a*   *e'lgwa'si·a Tco'meli· nadɑ'ŋgwus gi·saŋkwa'sit*
"Once   while I was asleep   dreaming   Joe Mary   my cousin   cooking

edali·na'mi·hɑn ka'i·ko'kuk ktaha'n·do amɔsla'bik·e¹ me''tci·ne nodawi'k'-
there I saw   in kettle   great magic   spider   dead."   Then he

hama'wɑn   wa'dɑŋk'ʷsal   elgwa''sit   nodado''kewɑn   udi''lɑn   koli·dəbi·-
wrote him   his cousin   what he dreamt   then he told him   he said   "You

na'wɑn   kəda'tawaŋkwa'zudi tci·ba'dok t·e kdali·na'mi·hɑn amɔslabi·'k·e
examine well   your cooking vessel   perhaps   then there you will see   spider."

Free Translation

"Once when I slept I dreamt that Joe Mali, my cousin, was cooking. Then I saw in the kettle a great magic spider lying dead."² In the meantime his cousin wrote a letter to him, telling him what he had dreamt, and he said, "You examine well the kettle in which you cook your food. Perhaps you will see a spider." (This letter was a fore-warning of the spider incident. Had he eaten the food he thinks that he would have been poisoned by it.)

The Shaman Disguised as a Porcupine (Penobscot)

A hunter and his partner were once away up the river trapping. They set their traps everywhere but had bad luck. When they looked after the traps they always found them sprung but couldn't find the cause. So one night they were sitting around their camp talking about their bad luck when they heard a noise outside and lo, there was a porcupine looking right in at them with a face like a man's. When he saw them staring at him the porcupine made off. Pretty soon the hunters heard another noise on the outside of their wigwam and looking up through the smoke-hole, beheld there the same porcupine peering down. Now they could see its place and it was the face of a man in their village. The older hunter took a big stick and threw it at the porcupine. It hit him in the face and

---

¹ Literally "net weaver."

² Newell Lion quoting old Joe Glossian.

he tumbled off and made away into the woods. "Now," said the hunter, "we will have good luck after this." That was a shaman. When they next visited their traps they found a good catch, and their luck continued good. When they got home they told their story and discovered that a certain man in the village had, as he claimed, met with an accident. He had his face disfigured. The hunters went up to see him and found that his face was broken just where he had been hit with the big stick.

A Dreamer Assumes the Form of a Ball of Fire[1] (Penobscot)

An old man and his son went hunting. His wife and daughter-in-law did not like to stay at home so they went with him. They built their camp out of boughs and made a fire in the midst of a shelter. The father and son went out hunting and left the women at the camp alone. They were to be back in three days, but at the end of three days they did not return. The son's wife got weary and did not know what kept them so long, since it was four or five days since they had gone. That night the mother-in-law who was very fond of smoking lay down near the fire to smoke. Her daughter-in-law was lying in one corner of the camp on the boughs. The old woman told the younger that she was going to sleep and dream about where the men were, and what they were doing. When she finished smoking she lay on her back. Finally the young woman saw a ball of fire come out of her mouth. She became very frightened. She jumped up and tried to arouse the old woman, she turned her on her side and shook her. Then she believed the old woman to be dead. The ball of fire that came from the old woman's mouth went round and round the camp and around the old woman. The young woman turned her over again and when she did so the ball of fire went back into the old woman's mouth. Then she began to move about. She said that she had had a long sleep. She said, "Don't worry they will be back tomorrow. They have had good luck and are bringing lots of game. I just saw them sitting by their fire eating supper." The next day the hunters appeared with an abundance of game of all sorts.

---

[1] Written by Katie Mitchell (1910).

INDEX TO VOLUME VI